FOREWORD

Classroom art ~~...~~ ivities to inspire students ~~...~~ arts and aid their devel~~...~~ The activities provide opportunities for directed skill development in the disciplines of drawing, painting and printmaking, while remaining largely open-ended, encouraging students to experiment and explore the possibilities of using their own unique techniques and ideas. The activities cover the use of a wide range of inexpensive media readily available in craft stores and schools and stimulate imagination by building from familiar ideas to an individual response.

Information to support the teacher includes:

* step-by-step pictorial instructions,

* ideas for inspiring the students,

* examples of finished artworks to use as a student stimulus,

* response questions to assist the students to analyse and appraise the skills used, the elements of art (line, shape, colour, pattern and texture) and the content of their own artwork and the artworks of others,

* variations and stimulus to provoke invention upon each activity,

* cross-curricular activity suggestions, and

* display suggestions.

Published 2004

ISBN-13 978-1-74126-108-0

CONTENTS

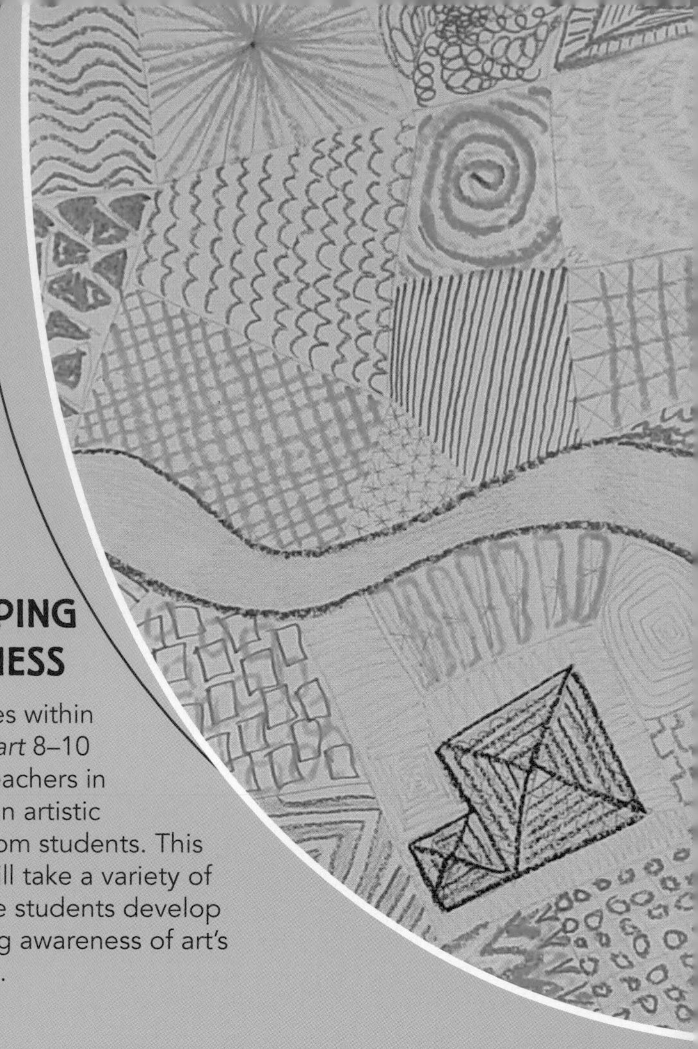

DEVELOPING AWARENESS

The activities within *Classroom art* 8–10 will assist teachers in extracting an artistic response from students. This response will take a variety of forms as the students develop a deepening awareness of art's possibilities.

Art:

- encourages imagination and the ability to solve problems and work within set parameters,
- provides opportunity for lateral and original thought where there are no boundaries dictated by what is 'right' or 'wrong' but simply by what is possible,
- provides a rare vehicle through which we can directly or indirectly communicate and make personal statements about who we are and the life we are living.

To understand and create art, both as a skill and a human response, students need to be aware of the way art is composed. By providing students with a broad cross-section of activities, the teacher will be equipped to introduce and explore each of the 'elements of art' that combine to form visual arts. These elements of art include:

- line,
- shape,
- colour,
- pattern, and
- texture.

Exposure to, and opportunities to exercise these elements, will provide students with the building blocks used by them and other artists to create images, project ideas and illusions, and describe atmosphere or 'tone' within an artwork. By developing artistic awareness in this way, students will be equipped to offer their own response with increased sensitivity.

ENCOURAGING CREATIVITY

In order to encourage creativity, the focus needs to be on individualism. All children make their own art in their own way. Art is one of the only disciplines where we are not required to compete against one another. In fact, the essence of producing art is in acquiring and demonstrating a different personal response – not the 'right' answer. Art is therefore something that everyone should participate in without fear.

However, students are often reluctant to participate in artistic activities for fear of producing substandard work. Because artwork is 'displayed', students may be left feeling exposed by their artwork. It is a good idea to start with more abstract styles to allow the students to build confidence in their ability to combine the elements of art in an informal way. Exposure to post modern artists and their work can also develop awareness that art is a means of expression through the art elements, colour, shape, line, pattern and texture, rather than a means of replicating an image. Though every artwork a student produces may not 'work', it can be viewed as part of a process towards creating a work that is pleasing. Students need to be aware that sometimes things don't 'look' right, but that their awareness of what looks 'good' demonstrates their artistic ability and can be used to guide future efforts. It is often through these 'mistakes' that new inventive techniques, ideas and effects are born.

After making art, the students should talk about their work and become aware of why they have created it in the way they have. Many students will be content to look at their artwork and the artwork of others purely aesthetically. Encourage them to consider whether they have used their art to tell a story or show how they feel. By considering the purpose of their artwork as a means of sharing something of themselves or what they think or believe, many students can be encouraged to see their own work and the work of others as valuable, and be inspired to reach their true potential.

MODELLING

Students who are told to draw something with no prior practice or information merely repeat the symbols they always draw. Modelling plays an integral role in developing confidence in new artists and providing them with the tools they need to broaden their artistic response. Art does not simply 'explode' onto a page. There are basic skills and techniques involved, just as with any discipline, which require teaching and practice. It is by applying these skills and techniques to new situations and adapting them to suit the needs of the artist, that the individuality and creativity of art can be expressed.

Step-by-step pictorial instructions accompany each of the activities in *Classroom art* 8–10. These instructions provide teachers with a simple, logical process to follow and direct their students. A larger photo of a finished artwork has been included as a standard stimulus for the students to aspire to, but not necessarily as a model to copy.

Each artwork in the book aims to develop a different skill or technique or addresses and explores a new concept or style. The purpose of each activity has been described under 'Indications' and should be made clear to the students prior to the lesson and reviewed during the modelling process as a focus for the students to practise and develop.

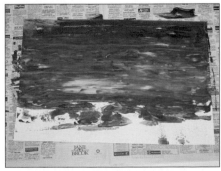
Step 1

Step 2

Step 3

Step-by-step instructions – 'Sunset silhouette', pp 46–47.

DEVELOPING SKILLS AND ENCOURAGING PRACTICE

Students love the success experienced by repeating and refining newly-learnt skills. Drawing, painting and printmaking techniques are no exception. It is often during skills-based activities that less confident art students will produce their most pleasing work and be inspired to branch out into more expressive ventures.

To be able to draw in different ways, students need to continue to explore drawing media in order to understand and use them for the special effects they wish to achieve. Allow the students time for 'discovery'. In practice sessions, include an element of exploration and an opportunity to develop a personal style. Challenge them with simple problem-solving tasks. For example, how many different types of marks can be made with a single medium? How many more can be created using two media? Can you create marks to represent different textures – spiky, crinkly, swirly, muddy or rough? Can you invent a new colour by mixing paints and what would you name it? What other tools can be used to apply paint? Provide the students with a broad range of media to explore, and apply them to a variety of surfaces. When developing new skills, allow the students plenty of time to create so they can gain skills by looking, sharing ideas and practising.

Often, students will spontaneously create a picture while practising new techniques. These artworks should be valued and used to demonstrate that art is a composition of art elements – not necessarily a recognisable picture. Encourage students to share and discuss these artworks in terms of both content and the skills or techniques they used to create an effect that pleases them.

APPRAISING ART

Appraising art is a skill requiring an ability to look at art with personal criteria in mind. In this way, appraisals will vary from one person to another and cannot be assessed as 'right or wrong'. Initially, students will appraise work instinctively, using a 'what looks good' criterion. As they develop an understanding of the elements of art and how they interact to form a balanced image, these too will become part of their criteria. Older students will also address moods, medium, technique appropriateness, content and the artist's purpose in their appraisals. By using these criteria, students will learn to address what kind of art it is, why it has been made, what it is about, what materials or media have been used, and what techniques and art elements have been incorporated. Appraising the work of others – peers, older students, local and famous artists – helps students identify why and how we make art.

It is equally important for the students to appraise their own work in this way and to share their work with others. Encourage the students to focus on what they have done, the materials and tools used, what they have learnt, and what could be done better next time. Address what elements of art are in their work, and why they are or are not happy with their artwork. Be aware, though, that it is also acceptable not to discuss our own work. Sometimes our art is just for us.

Practising parallel line texture –'Broken line bugs', pp 4–5.

CLASSROOM ORGANISATION

The environment in which the students create their artwork needs to be a balance of stimulation and organisation. A room with plenty of stimulus, artworks created by other artists and students, bright colours and elaborate displays, will inspire the students' to stretch the boundaries of their ideas. However, a room that is too busy may crowd the students' thinking and prevent them from developing their own ideas, as so many are already on show to choose from. An environment that is neatly presented with stimulating displays is most effective. A well-presented workspace will also encourage the students to take pride in their personal work area and participate more readily in cleaning-up tasks.

Areas used for art can quickly become disaster areas. There should be a designated place for art media, brushes and tools, water containers with broad heavy bases, palettes, paper and cleaning equipment. Ensure the students know these places and are made responsible for their care. In this way, the students will be more particular and conservative with their use of valuable resources.

Ensure the students have their own painting shirt and that there is a ready supply of 'spares' for those that do not have one. A rubbish bag with head and armholes cut out makes an excellent makeshift painting shirt. Always insist upon the students wearing their painting shirts while cleaning up, as this is where most accidental drips and hand prints take place. Before messy art activities, cover the work surface with newspaper, which can be thrown away afterwards, or invest in cheap plastic drop sheets to use as cover-ups. Buckets with damp sponges, dry rags and soda water (for getting paint stains out of carpet and clothing) should also be on hand during messy activities, ready for unexpected spills.

SAFETY

Some art techniques and processes require the use of materials such as bleach and lit candles that may be harmful to the students if used incorrectly. Using these materials with lower primary students is not recommended. They should only be used in closely supervised situations with older students or adult assistance. Potentially dangerous materials have not been used in any activities in *Classroom art* 8–10.

Many art and craft media are toxic or lead-based and care should be taken when ordering or purchasing art supplies to ensure that they are non-toxic and safe for children.

Supervision is essential when students are using scissors or any sharp tools. The most common occurrences of accidents and injury are during the cleaning-up process. Provide a closely monitored, controlled environment in which the students can conduct cleaning tasks safely.

Activities involving materials such as bleach should be undertaken in well-ventilated areas.

PARENTAL INVOLVEMENT

Art activities involving students can be more successful if adequate adult help is available. Parents are an invaluable part of classroom organisation. Establish a group of willing parents to become regulars with art activities. Orientate them with classroom organisation and clean-up procedures. Allocate a number of students to each adult. Ask helpers to assist in providing and maintaining their group's resources, review instructions with the students and accompany them to designated clean-up tasks. Encourage the parents to create their own art if they would like to, and to model their thought process as they create. Always make a point of showing appreciation for parents who have taken time out to assist you and your students.

ASSESSMENT

Assessment of artworks created by students must be objective and the criteria by which they will be assessed made clear to the students before they create their artwork. Students must also be given the opportunity to reflect upon and discuss their own artwork and the artwork of others in order to demonstrate their understanding of art.

Ideally, assessment of visual arts should be made in four areas:

- ability to identify and discuss art ideas,

- demonstration of art skills, techniques and processes,

- response to visual arts through reflection and evaluation, and

- understanding the role of visual arts in society.

To evaluate a student's understanding and ability as an artist comprehensively, teachers may need to make use of a range of assessment tools, including observations, discussion transcripts and the artworks themselves. An art portfolio can be initiated and built over time to include examples of the student's developing skills, artistic responses and photos of finished pieces. The students will enjoy reflecting upon earlier artworks and monitoring their own development.

DISPLAY IDEAS

Classroom art displays can be used to create an atmosphere to enhance learning and encourage an awareness of how the elements of art, such as colour and pattern, can affect us and reflect the world around us. Clear, vibrant presentation will bring professionalism to the students' work and add value to their art.

Displays can be enhanced using materials in colours that support the artwork. Colours associated with the art's theme, simple frames set against a stark black background, or the use of many shades of one colour to increase vibrancy, are some methods used to enhance an artwork. Positioning the display in a prominent position in the room or using focused lighting will also add effect.

When developing a class display, involve the students in the process. Discuss whether the finished display looks good or how it could be made to look better, how it is positioned and how the art has been spaced, whether the background is appropriate and enhances the artwork, whether the mounts distract the eye from the art, what additions could be made to bring meaning to the art, or what text could be added.

Individual students' work can also be made a focus for display. By incorporating an 'artwork of the week' into the room, students can be encouraged to appraise their own art and learn to listen to others as they discuss their work and ask questions. When selecting a 'picture of the week', discuss why the picture was chosen and put up a sign describing the work and the reasons it was chosen.

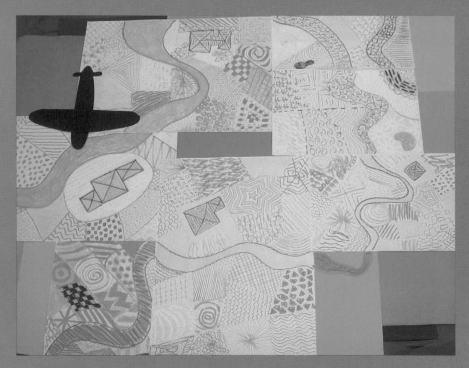

Class display – 'Mountains high and rivers deep', pp 50–51.

UNDERSTANDING THE COLOUR WHEEL

Understanding colours, the effects they can create when placed against each other and how they mix to create new colours, is integral to creating pleasing artwork and displays. The following is an outline of the 'basics' of colour.

Primary colours

– yellow, blue, red.

Primary colours can be mixed to create all other base colours except black and white.

Tints

– adding white

Tints can be created by adding white to any base colour. Tints are commonly referred to as 'pastel' colours. Large quantities of white are required to significantly tint a base colour.

Shades

– adding black

Shades can be created by adding black to any base colour. Small quantities of black paint are required to make a base colour significantly darker.

Secondary colours

– green, orange, purple.

Secondary colours are created when two primary colours are mixed.

red + yellow = orange
yellow + blue = green
blue + red = purple

By adding more of one primary colour than the other, variations of a secondary colour can be made. For example, a small amount of yellow and a large amount of blue will make a blue-green colour. Adding black or white to two primary colours will create tints and shades of secondary colours.

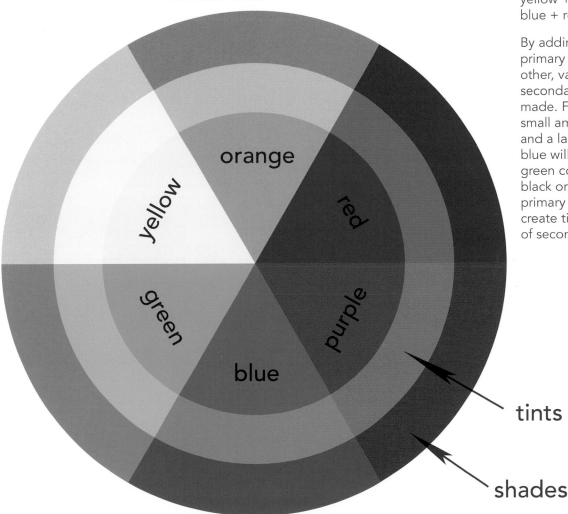

tints

shades

Tertiary colours

are created when any combination of three primary colours is mixed together.

When all three primary colours are mixed, variations of brown can be achieved by adding more or less of each colour. A chocolate brown colour can be made by combining equal parts of red and yellow and a very small amount of blue.

Complementary colours are those

which are opposite on the colour wheel and which stand out strongly when placed against one another. Examples of complementary colours are orange and blue, green and red and purple and yellow.

Analogous colours

Analogous colours describe those that exist side by side on the colour wheel. Artworks in analogous colours are generally composed in variations of two or three colours found side by side on the colour wheel; for example, blue, green and yellow.

RESOURCES

Colour media

lead pencil
coloured pencils
greasy crayons
fluorescent crayons
metallic crayons
felt-tipped pens
marking pens
black fine-tipped pen
acrylic paints
fluorescent paints
powdered tempera paint
edicol powder (dye)
food colouring
pastels

Other resources

foil
strong glue
ruler
toothpicks
paintbrushes of various thicknesses
newspaper
scissors
coloured paper squares
picture or photocopy of a textured object to copy
candles
white art paper
matches
coloured mounting card
liquid starch
straw
silver and gold glitter
sponges
toothbrushes
still-life subject
magazines
round objects to trace
shells
patterned and textured paper
thick cardboard squares
thin soft rope
clay
tennis ball
screen
squeegee
materials for making a collage
heavy cardboard
bleach
tray
etching tools
textured fabric scraps
hard roller
soft roller
paint palette
sand
buff card
absorbent paper towels
straw
glass
black paper
leaves
gloves
cardboard tubes

INDICATIONS

Indications specific to each activity are provided. Each covers one of the following areas:

- skills, techniques and processes, and
- responding, reflecting on and evaluating visual arts.

SEEKING INSPIRATION

We are surrounded by stimuli. Becoming inspired to transform a stimulus into art requires a process by which the stimulus is sparked into an original idea worthy of expressing. This process may take place simply through quiet thought where a mental 'domino effect' will lead a simple stimulus to a different creative level.

However, in a classroom situation, it is often through discussion with others that original ideas are triggered. Therefore, for most art students, discussion is valuable and should not be discouraged.

Students should be encouraged to discuss why the pictures we draw or paint are different from photographs, to compare illustration styles, and the difference between real and abstract pictures. Students should also be encouraged to attempt to replicate the techniques used by other artists, watch artists work and to discuss art with artists themselves.

Teachers should expose the students to artworks that they are enthusiastic about themselves, and demonstrate a broad selection of styles and periods. This will provide discussion opportunities relating to specific artists, styles or movements, content, media and art elements; all of which provide key material from which students can develop interest and artistic direction.

Discussion, personal experiences and exposure to collections of art stimuli relating to a particular theme or style will provide a range of ideas for students to mesh into a new and unique idea for their own artwork.

Collections may include artworks or displays from other classrooms, prints, pictures in books, photographs, tools and media, photos, magazine articles, posters, artefacts, everyday objects, journal entries, poems, and other artists' work.

Each activity within *Classroom art* 8–10 is prefaced by a list of ideas that can be used to inspire student interest in readiness for the activity.

INSTRUCTIONS

Specific four-step instructions are given for each activity, with accompanying photographs.

REFLECTION QUESTIONS encourage students to evaluate the skills, techniques and processes used and extend students' thoughts concerning the use of the technique or subject, in order to appraise their art.

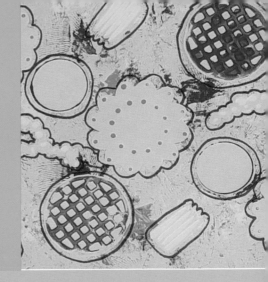

VARIATIONS

When students are using new techniques or responding to a new stimulus, there will always be opportunities for numerous variations on a theme. These variation activities will allow students to consolidate what they have learnt and will also demonstrate how a technique, idea or style can be altered to produce a different response. Students will often spontaneously see an opportunity for producing something unique from an activity, either prior to commencing or during the process of creating an artwork. Teachers should always allow the students to deviate and develop their creative response. There will be time for specific skill development later. Though technique is important, creativity should always take priority.

A list of suggested variations supplements each of the activities in *Classroom art* 8–10.

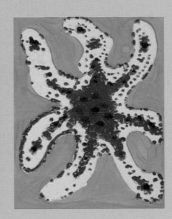

ACROSS THE CURRICULUM

Art is a wonderful means of expressing new discoveries and personal interests. Students learning new material in other curriculum areas will find art a stimulating means of expressing their new knowledge. Emersion within a theme or topic will provide ample stimulus for new and creative artwork. Although there is merit in teaching art in isolation for 'art's sake', in a classroom situation, student involvement in other areas of the curriculum can be utilised to form a foundation for original art ideas.

Each activity in *Classroom art* 8–10 is accompanied by a list of suggested cross-curricular activities. These activities can be used to consolidate or complement learning in art lessons.

RECIPES FOR MEDIA

Liquid starch – Dissolve starch powder in a small amount of cold water to make a paste. Add boiling water, stirring continuously until the mixture becomes opaque and of the desired consistency. Create a thinner consistency for paint or a thicker consistency for use as a glue.

Liquid starch is suitable for gluing paper, sticks to metal, glass, waxed paper and plastic, and dries clear. Add edicol dye or powdered tempera paint to liquid starch to create a thicker, slightly translucent paint ideal for finger painting. Adding liquid starch to paint is an economical way to increase paint supplies and will keep for long periods in airtight containers in the refrigerator.

Cornflour paste – Use two tablespoons of cornflour to one cup of water. Mix enough water with the cornflour to make a paste. Add the remaining water and bring to the boil. Continue to stir until a custard-like consistency is achieved. Add water if a thinner consistency is preferred. Mix powdered tempera paints or edicol dye with a small amount of water and add to the mixture when cool.

Cornflour paste is suitable for gluing paper or for adding to edicol or powdered paint.

Edicol paint – Dissolve about 1/8 of a teaspoon of edicol dye powder in a tablespoon of water and add to cornflour paste, commercially available wallpaper paste or liquid starch to create thick translucent paint in brilliant colours. Add detergent to the mixture to assist in adhesion to glass, plastics and foil. Mix edicol powder with small amounts of water to create vivid dyes for use on fabric or paper. Food colouring can be used as an inexpensive, but less vivid, substitute for edicol dye.

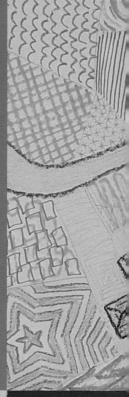

Powdered tempera paint – Dissolve a teaspoon of powdered tempera paint in a small amount of water to make a paste. Add to cornflour paste, commercially available wallpaper paste or liquid starch to create a thick, opaque paint suitable for covering patterned surfaces, such as lettering on boxes.

Soap paint – Pour two cups of warm water into a bowl. Using an electric mixer, begin mixing, adding soap flakes gradually. Beat until the soap forms soft peaks. Add colouring to the soap and mix through. Powdered tempera paint, edicol paint or acrylic paint can be used to colour soap paint successfully.

Drawing

Resources
- white paper
- coloured felt-tipped pens
- coloured card for mounting
- glue
- lead pencil
- scissors

Indications:

Skills, techniques, technologies and processes

- Controls a pencil to form closed flowing shapes.
- Colours within a boundary.
- Cuts carefully around the exterior boundary of a shape.

Responding, reflecting on and evaluating visual arts:

- Enjoys creating imagined shapes.
- Freely experiments with shape.
- Makes individual choices.

Inspiration

- Students make sandcastles by dripping wet sand. Note the sloppy patterns and shapes created.
- Discuss closed and open shapes, large and small shapes and shapes that are 'fluid' or rigid.
- Allow the students to practise drawing fluid lines and shapes.

Instructions

Step 1

Use a lead pencil to draw fluid 'blob' shapes. Add new shapes to those already drawn to create closed shapes spreading across the page. Encourage the students to use a combination of large and small, fat and thin shapes. Do not leave any gaps between the shapes.

Step 2

Select seven different coloured felt-tipped pens. These can all be variations of one or two colours or can span the spectrum of colours. Trace around each shape, alternating between the seven colours chosen.

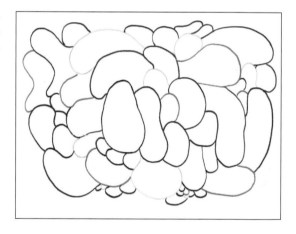

Step 3

Randomly choose seven 'blobs' to colour. Consider how you can 'balance' the picture by choosing blobs from all parts of the picture rather than in one area. Colour the chosen shapes by using either one colour for each chosen shape, or a complete rainbow of colours within each chosen shape.

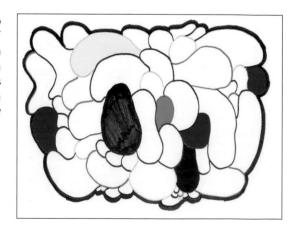

Connecting blobs

Step 4   Cut around the perimeter of the blob shape ready for mounting. Glue sparingly to attach the 'blob' picture to red or other brightly-coloured card. The mounting card should complement the colours used on the random blobs.

Reflection questions

- How would you describe the shapes you drew?
- Does your blob drawing look like anything you have seen before?
- Why did you choose to colour the shapes this way? Why did you think that would look good?

Variations

- Use blobs to make up an image of something familiar, e.g. a blob puppy.
- Make a 'blob' style drawing using more rigid shapes.
- Use analogous colours (colours next to each other on the colour wheel) to colour all shapes in the blob drawing.
- Trace over the blob shapes using a felt-tipped pen to help the pattern stand out.

Cross-curricular activities

- Use blocks to measure the area of large irregular blob shapes drawn on butcher's paper. Count the number of blocks used and compare to other blob shapes measured.
- Students pretend they are 'blobs' morphing into different letter shapes.
- Use plasticine to make a given number of 'blobby' body parts.
- Make caterpillars using a set number of blobs.

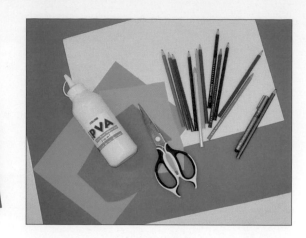

Resources

- coloured pencils
- green card for mounting
- different shades of green coloured paper
- fine-tipped black pen or coloured felt-tipped pens
- scissors and glue
- white paper
- lead pencil

Indications:

Skills, techniques, technologies and processes

- Draws parallel lines to create the illusion of texture.
- Incorporates straight and curvy lines among parallel texture lines.

Responding, reflecting on and evaluating visual arts

- Appreciates that the direction and proximity of lines can combine to create texture.
- Understands that broken lines can be used to describe the outline of a shape.

Inspiration

- Students practise drawing dotted lines.
- Look at close-up pictures of animal fur or hair to see the way lines can be drawn parallel to create a furry edge.
- Provide a live pet such as a rabbit or guinea pig for the students to handle and look at the fur.

Instructions

Step 1

Provide the students with scrap paper to practise drawing different kinds of broken lines. Encourage them to experiment with dotted lines, broken lines which are tall, short, sloping, wavy, becoming wider, becoming narrower and so on. Ask the students to think about where broken lines could be used in drawing, instead of straight lines.

Step 2

Allow the students to combine some of the broken lines they have been experimenting with to create the outline and main features of an imaginary creature. Direct students to incorporate some 'normal' lines into their drawings to contrast with the broken lines, or to draw special features. The students should be given the freedom to draw as many or few creatures as they like and to think creatively about their size and form.

Step 3

Colour each of the creatures using unusual combinations of colours. The students can choose to trace their broken line outline with felt-tipped coloured pens or a black fine-tipped pen to help their creatures stand out. Cut out the creatures ready for mounting.

Broken line bugs

Step 4   Onto a piece of green card, glue a variety of leaf-shaped lengths of green paper to create a 'grass forest' for the creatures to live in. Glue the creatures into the grass forest so that some of the grass is in front of the creatures. Mount on a green background.

Reflection questions
- How did you make your creatures look furry?
- Did you use any 'normal' lines (not parallel) in your creatures? What parts did you use them for?
- Did your furry creatures end up looking like anything you had seen before?
- Were you happy with the way you coloured your furry creatures?

Variations
- Attempt to draw entire pictures, filling the page with nothing but lines. Explore with long, short, thick and thin lines.
- Draw line pictures using different media (pen, pencil, crayon).
- Draw line patterns to create optical illusions. Use bright colours to fill in the spaces created by the intersecting lines.

Cross-curricular activities
- Investigate how different textures feel.
- Draw letters, number shapes and patterns into a tray of sand.
- Explore the sense of touch. Provide a variety of objects for the students to guess by feeling each inside a 'feely' bag.
- Classify a group of objects by the way they feel, e.g. smooth, furry or bumpy.
- Investigate different animal coverings.

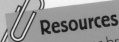

Resources
- green or brown card for mounting
- drawing media in shades of blue, green and brown
- white paper

Indications:

Skills, techniques, technologies and processes

- Draws imaginative patterns including radiating, rotational, and linear patterns.
- Uses a variety of media to create patterns.

Responding, reflecting on and evaluating visual arts

- Enjoys experimenting with a variety of mediums and determines preferences for each task.
- Appreciates that art can be taken from a range of perspectives.

Inspiration

- Look at aerial photographs of farming areas. Note how the land is divided up by its owners and takes on different colours according to what crops are being grown.
- Allow the students to experiment with a variety of drawing media and colours. Students choose the best to use in their own artwork to portray farmland.

Instructions

Step 1

Students imagine what a farm might look like from a 'bird's-eye' view. Instruct the students to draw a winding river across the page. Students draw a farmhouse on an appropriate section of the river bank. Ensure that the farmhouse is drawn as though looking from above.

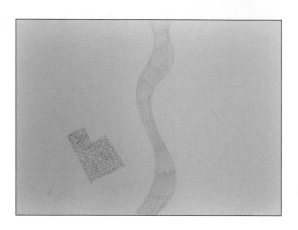

Step 2

Draw a patchwork of fields across the remainder of the page. These should not all be evenly spaced and sized. Refer the students back to aerial photographs of farmland and the irregularity of the patterns formed by the fields.

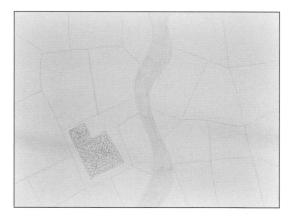

Step 3

In each 'field', attempt to create a pattern which is unique from all the other fields. This can be achieved by alternating between the media used or combining media within a field. Examples of patterns to experiment with include patterns radiating from a central point, linear patterns, patterns in arrays, concentric patterns and patterns which are symmetrically rotational. Each of these styles could be modelled for the students, to assist them in generating their own original version.

Bird's-eye view

Step 4 Choose green or brown card to mount the artwork. This will accentuate the contrast between the 'crops' and the farmhouse. Alternatively, place all the students' work side by side to create a class display of farming land. Make a black cut-out of a plane (from a bird's-eye view) to place across the class display, to indicate the drawings represent an aerial view.

Reflection questions

- What colours and media stand out most in your picture?
- Would someone else looking at your picture recognise it as depicting farmland from a 'bird's-eye' view? Why?
- What other subjects would be interesting from a 'bird's-eye' view?

Variations

- Use materials to create a collage of a farm using different textures of fabric to portray the different fields.
- Draw a bird or plane with a background of farmland or another type of environment.
- Use squares of coloured paper to make an airfield with a black strip for a runway. Use model planes to enhance the artwork.

Cross-curricular activities

- Discuss what it would be like to be a bird. Students write descriptions of what a bird might see from the sky.
- Make, continue and complete linear and array patterns.
- Find out about crops grown on farms and what the crops are used to make. For example; wheat → flour → bread.

Resources

- charcoal
- white paper
- red, orange and yellow paper squares
- black card for mounting
- scissors
- glue

Indications:

Skills, techniques, technologies and processes

- Manipulates charcoal into a comfortable grip for drawing.
- Makes a variety of markings with charcoal to create a range of effects.

Responding, reflecting on and evaluating visual arts

- Appreciates that using a more primitive medium such as charcoal, can suit specific subject matter.
- Enjoys experimenting with a new 'grip' and new techniques using an alternative medium.

Inspiration

- Discuss where charcoal comes from. Investigate other naturally-occurring media and how indigenous people have used them to create traditional artwork.
- Look at artworks by indigenous people around the world.
- Discuss and imagine what a landscape might look like after a fire has burnt it.

Instructions

Step 1

Discuss where charcoal comes from and what the students know about the properties and texture of charcoal. Students handle charcoal and attempt to draw onto scrap paper prior to beginning their drawings.

Explain that the students will be drawing a forest of burnt trees. Discuss what this might look like, and the sketchy lines and shapes that might be found in this kind of drawing. Demonstrate how drawing trees higher and shorter on the page makes them look further away, than trees drawn lower and taller. Discuss how trees drawn in different places and of different sizes can combine to create a forest where some trees are in the distance and some are close up.

Students sketch their charcoal forest, making sure to include trees that are closer and further away. Encourage them to also include some burnt twigs and ground matter in their drawings.

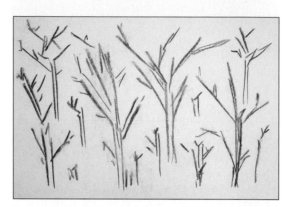

Step 2

Students create 'smoke' in their drawings by using their fingers to smudge sections of the trees. They may need to redraw some parts of the trees to regain their original definition.

Step 3

Cut out flame shapes from orange, red and yellow coloured paper.

Step 4   Arrange the coloured paper flames onto the drawing and glue them down accordingly. Mount the finished artwork onto a black background. Alternatively, all of the students' pictures can be mounted side by side to create a burnt forest frieze.

Reflection questions

- How did the charcoal feel to draw with? How is it different from using pencil?
- Did you hold the charcoal differently to a pencil when you used it to draw?
- Did the charcoal draw the way you wanted it to? How did this affect the image you were trying to create?
- Were you satisfied with the 'burnt' appearance of your final artwork?

Variations

- Use charcoal to draw simple pictures on paper or card with different textures.
- Use charcoal to make rubbings of things in the natural environment.
- Use the unique qualities of charcoal to enhance other artworks. For example, use charcoal to smudge clouds in the sky or to make a striking black border or outline.

Cross-curricular activities

- Investigate how forests regenerate after a fire.
- Discuss and review fire safety procedures.
- Investigate climatic conditions that are conducive to bushfires.
- Discuss flammable and inflammable products.

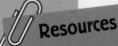
Resources

- toy
- coloured pencils
- coloured card for mounting
- white paper
- lead pencil

Indications:

Skills, techniques, technologies and processes

- Draws a familiar inanimate object.
- Includes realistic colours and details in a still life drawing.

Responding, reflecting on and evaluating visual arts

- Identifies differences between their own still life drawing and what is seen and attempts to rectify the differences.
- Assesses their still life artwork in terms of how realistic it looks.

Inspiration

- Appraise still life drawings such as *Apples and oranges* by Cezanne (1895).
- Students bring in a special toy from home. Encourage the students to look at their toy closely, and then, without showing the toy to the class, give a description of it for the students to guess.
- Discuss how a still life is different from a landscape or portrait.

Instructions

Step 1

Discuss what is meant by a still life (the drawing of an inanimate object). Students study their toy closely, looking for the shapes from which it is made and the proportions of each part in relation to other parts. Ask the students to look at the space around the toy and imagine that the toy is a two-dimensional cut-out. What shape does it leave if cut away? Discuss how the students might go about making sure their toy is drawn in proportion and fills the page. What parts of the toy should they draw first? Last?

Allow the students to roughly sketch the general outline of their toy onto a blank page, considering what they have discussed. The students should be encouraged to sketch lightly in coloured pencils and then to retrace the final outline when they are happy with their sketch.

Step 2

Colour the drawing using colours as close as possible to the actual toy. The students should be guided to see areas of shadow and to colour these areas more heavily or with a darker coloured pencil.

Step 3

Students consider a background for their picture. Their goal for this exercise should be not to draw what is actually in the background but to choose colours that will make their drawing look clean, 'new' and appealing. Students complete their background, colouring from the toy outline outwards.

Still life toy

Step 4

Students choose coloured card to mount their still life that will draw attention to the colours in the toy rather than to the background of the picture. As a rule, this will be achieved by selecting the most dominant colour in the subject of the picture. Hang the drawings along the wall to create a mini 'art gallery'. Students can take on the role of art critic and express the reasons for their personal 'still life' preferences.

Reflection questions

- Did you choose a suitable toy to draw? Why was it a good or a poor choice?
- Were you able to use colours that matched the colours in your toy? How did this affect your drawing?
- Can you see parts of your drawing where the shapes aren't quite right? How do the shapes need to change to look right?

Variations

- Draw other familiar objects such as a shoe, bike, tree, flowers or food.
- Draw portraits and profiles of other students in the class.
- Use other media such as lead pencils or pastels to draw pictures from still life..

Cross-curricular activities

- Investigate the properties and features of a variety of toys. Include toys with moving parts, remote controlled toys and toys that make noises.
- Students design the 'ultimate' toy. Draw diagrams labelled with its special features.
- Compare a toy for a baby with a toy for a teenager. Discuss why they are different.

Drawing

Resources
- four squares of white paper
- white scrap paper
- felt-tipped pens
- black card for mounting
- ruler
- scissors

Indications:

Skills, techniques, technologies and processes

- Uses lines, shapes and colours to describe emotions.
- Responds to personal feelings and experiences through art.

Responding, reflecting on and evaluating visual arts

- Recognises that colours can evoke particular emotions.
- Understands that colour, line and shape can combine to give an image a 'tone' or atmosphere.

Inspiration

- Share stories about things that make the students feel different emotions.
- Make different lines, colours, shapes and patterns on a page for the students to discuss and decide what emotions they could represent.
- Look at pictures that evoke particular emotions (fear, sorrow, joy). Discuss the colours and styles used and how they work together to create these feelings.

Instructions

Step 1

Cut out four squares of white paper of equal size. These can be prepared for the students prior to the lesson or can be measured with a ruler and cut out by the students.

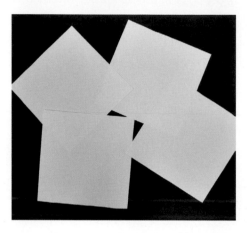

Step 2

Brainstorm a list of feelings. Discuss how these words might be written to show the emotion of the word. Allow the students to choose four feelings to write in each of the squares. The students may choose to use decorative writing for the words.

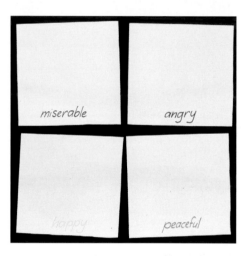

Step 3

On a separate sheet of scrap paper, allow the students to experiment with colours, lines, shapes and patterns to determine what they think would best illustrate each of the feelings. For example, a happy feeling might be portrayed in bright yellow flower shapes and flowing wavy orange or red lines. A sad feeling might be illustrated in dark colours using down-turned shapes and thick flat lines. Allow the students to portray each of the feelings they chose in this way, thinking carefully about the colours they choose and the shapes and lines they create on the page. It may help them to think of a time they felt that way. Their drawing should be an emotional response.

Colours and feelings

Step 4 Mount the four 'feelings' onto a large square of black card. Alternatively, combine all the students' pictures randomly onto a large display board so that they appear to be scattered over the wall. Add items such as a party hat, that remind us of certain feelings (happiness, excitement).

Reflection questions

- What feelings did you choose? Why did you choose these feelings to draw?
- What did you think about while you were drawing each of the designs?
- Are there any parts of your designs that you feel are not quite appropriate? Why?
- Where could you use designs like these in real life?

Variations

- Cover a box with white paper and design packaging for a product of your choice using suitable, appealing colours and styles.
- Make advertising posters or flyers that make a person 'feel' a certain way.
- Design greeting cards for different occasions where the colours and patterns suit the tone of the card.

Cross-curricular activities

- Read and discuss stories that evoke particular emotions.
- Learn and sing songs that are sad or happy.
- Listen to a variety of music. Students describe how the music made them feel.
- Encourage the students to share emotional experiences they have had.
- Investigate non-verbal communication that describes different emotions.

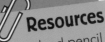

Resources
- lead pencil
- maroon card for mounting
- two sheets of heavy white paper or card
- green and blue paint
- coloured greasy crayons
- coloured felt-tipped pens
- toothpicks
- scissors and strong glue

Indications:

Skills, techniques, technologies and processes

- Draws a reflected image.
- Combines printing, etching, drawing, painting and colouring to produce a unique mixed-media image.

Responding, reflecting on and evaluating visual arts

- Understands that reflected images are not necessarily symmetrical.
- Appreciates that the length of shadows and choice of colours combine to describe different times of the day.

Inspiration

- Watch how shadows move and change over a day.
- Look at pictures of sunsets and sunrises. Note the colours that occur naturally in the sky at different times of the day.
- Make 'people' shadows against a wall by shining a torch.
- Use a torch shining on a figurine to observe the changes to the shadow.

Instructions

Step 1

Fold a sheet of heavy art paper or white card in half. Place the paper so the fold line is at the bottom. From the fold line, draw a few tree shapes. Encourage the students to think of different types of trees they know of to replicate. Discuss the colours of leaves at different times of the year. Students should choose 'autumn' coloured felt-tipped pens to colour their trees.

Unfold the sheet of paper. Starting from the fold line, cut around the tree shapes leaving the bottom of the sheet intact. Fold the trees into a standing position. Glue the half sheet with the tree shapes to the second sheet of card or heavy paper so the trees are standing in the middle of the second sheet. (The trees will remain unglued.) Allow the glue the dry.

Step 2

Using greasy crayons, completely cover the base in patches of autumn colours. Fold the trees out of the way where necessary.

Step 3

Paint the top half of the paper in green to represent a shadowy background. While the paint is still wet, allow the trees to fall backwards into the green paint to coat the backs of the trees. When the trees are carefully lifted from the paint they will leave an impression which will represent shadows. When dry, paint the bottom half blue to represent the water into which the trees will reflect.

Step 4

When the blue paint is dry, place the artwork in the sun or into a position where a shadow is being clearly cast by the upright trees onto the blue half of the paper. The shadows should be elongated or distorted in some way to give the best effect. Use a toothpick to scratch away the paint where the shadows are being cast to create a 'reflection' of each tree in the water. Mount on a maroon background. If the paper used is thin or becomes weakened with colouring, sticky tape can be used to hold the trees in an upright position.

Reflection questions

- How did you try to create the impression of a reflection in water? How might you have done this differently or better?
- What time of day did you attempt to simulate in your picture?
- How did you try to give this impression?
- Was it easy to see and trace the shadow of the trees you cut out? What difficulties did you encounter?

Variations

- Students write their name in flowing writing along the folded edge of a sheet of paper. They hold the folded paper (with the printed side to the back) up to the window or other light source and trace the mirror image of their name. The paper is then unfolded and coloured to create a personal totem pole.
- Students attempt to draw shadows to give drawings a three-dimensional quality.
- Make shadow puppets and perform a short play.

Cross-curricular activities

- Make shadow puppets and re-enact a favourite story using an overhead projector.
- Investigate symmetry. Identify symmetrical shapes and shapes with rotational symmetry.
- Make a sundial and mark or read different times of the day.
- Note how the sun moves across the sky. Use a three-dimensional model to demonstrate how the earth moves around the sun.

Resources

- giraffe template made from thick card
- black fine-tipped pen
- lead pencil
- yellow, brown and orange felt-tipped pens
- purple and orange card for mounting
- white paper
- aluminium foil
- scissors and glue

Indications:

Skills, techniques, technologies and processes

- Traces a template in a variety of positions to create the illusion of movement.
- Cuts carefully and analyses overlapping lines to determine internal spaces.

Responding, reflecting on and evaluating visual arts

- Understands that an illusion of movement can be created in a still drawing.
- Appreciates that a single drawing has the ability to tell a story.

Inspiration

- Look at pictures of giraffes in the wild. Students discuss and imagine what a giraffe might 'dance' like.
- Read *Giraffes can't dance* by Giles Andreae and Guy Parker-Rees.
- Discuss colours that might be appropriate and look at the colours used by Guy Parker-Rees in his illustrations in the book.

Instructions

Step 1

Find a picture of a giraffe in a leaping or running pose. You might find one in a book, magazine or on an Internet website. Use the illustration as a reference to draw the giraffe on thick card. Carefully cut around the shape ready for use as a template.

Students should think about how they could give the illusion of the giraffe leaping or dancing across the page. Encourage them to move their template in different positions across the page to help them visualise the 'leap' they will create. Allow the students to carefully trace around their template in the first position.

Step 2

Direct the students to check again where the other tracings will sit on the page in relation to their first tracing. Allow the students to trace their giraffe a further three times across the page in a 'leap' as planned.

Step 3

Ask the students to select felt-tipped pens in 'giraffe' colours. Colour each giraffe in one of these colours leaving the overlapping sections white. The students may also wish to trace around their giraffe shapes in black fine-tipped pen.

Giraffe dance

Step 4   Carefully cut around the exterior of the four giraffes and glue onto purple card. Mount onto an orange background. Make a round moon and stars by folding and shaping aluminium foil. Glue these to the card. Encourage the students to be creative when placing the moon and stars, and to consider viewing and using the frame as part of the picture.

Reflection questions

- What emotions would you like your drawing to make the viewer feel? Do you think you have achieved this?
- What impression do the overlapping legs of the giraffe give?
- Does your picture give the illusion of movement or dancing? How could you have enhanced this?

Variations

- Overlap a series of different shapes that are transparent, such as raindrops or bubbles, to give the picture a more translucent effect.
- Use pastel colours to colour the shapes created in the drawing to give a 'softer' finish.

Cross-curricular activities

- Students create a short African-style dance to a set piece of music and perform it for the class.
- Research an exotic animal and report back to the class.
- Discuss special days and celebrations in other cultures.
- Locate Africa on a world map. Find out where other exotic animals can be found in the world.
- Research endangered animals.

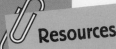

DRAWING

CLASSROOM ART
18
R.I.C. Publications

Resources
- white paper
- coloured felt-tipped pens
- lead pencil
- brightly coloured card for mounting
- blindfolds (optional)

Indications:

Skills, techniques, technologies and processes

- Draws marks on a page to represent what is felt with fingertips while blindfolded.

- Chooses fauve colours that are complementary and vibrant.

Responding, reflecting on and evaluating visual arts

- Appreciates drawing as a means of expressing something through the senses.

- Understands that different art styles exist and have definable characteristics.

Inspiration

- Look at fauve paintings such as *The sorrows of the king*, by Matisse (1952). Note the bright flat colours used.

- Discuss the way facial features have been 'mixed up' in paintings such as *Girl before a mirror*, by Picasso (1932).

- Try to identify a peer while blindfolded, using the sense of touch.

Instructions

Step 1

Explain to the students they are going to wear a blindfold and will draw only what they can feel. Allow the students to choose a partner whose face they will feel and draw. Alternatively, the students can feel and draw his/her own face, but will need a second person to hold the paper still while they draw. Ask the students to feel the boundaries of their page and the boundaries of their model's face, then proceed to draw the outline and features they can feel of their model. Students remove the blindfold and view their drawings. Emphasise there are no right or wrong drawing attempts, and, that in this style of drawing, the more 'wayward' it is the more interesting the final piece will be.

Step 2

Discuss what is meant by a 'closed' shape. Explain that to colour the drawing so the features can be defined, it will need to be altered to create a series of closed shapes. Demonstrate how a drawing can be altered in this way and then allow the students to create closed shapes from the lines and shapes they have drawn.

Step 3

Students use boldly coloured felt-tipped pens to colour the shapes they created. Emphasise that the picture is not intended to be realistic. Their aim should be to create a bright bold image, using colours which complement and contrast strongly with each other.

Unseen portrait

Step 4

Encourage the students to choose a colour within their drawing which stands out and to match this colour with a mount for their drawing.

Reflection questions

- How did your drawing turn out? Did it look the way you expected it to look when you opened your eyes?
- What did the strange looking face make you think of?
- Did your drawing still look like a face?
- Look at the shapes you created. How would you describe them?
- Are you pleased with the finished product?

Variations

- Draw, colour and cut out a number of facial features and use them to make a collage on brightly coloured paper.
- Draw several straight, curved or zig-zagged lines in black felt-tipped pen across the page so they intersect. Colour the shapes created using bright fauve colours. Frame the artwork in a bold colour. Title it with the name of an emotion such as 'Surprise!'

Cross-curricular activities

- Write a personal profile to accompany a self-portrait.
- Review the life of a famous person and write a short biography.
- Introduce the terms 'biography' and 'autobiography'. Look where these kinds of books can be found in the library.
- Solve 'mixed-up' puzzles or problems.

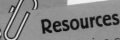

Resources

- magazine cuttings
- white paper
- coloured card for mounting
- coloured felt-tipped pens and/or coloured pencils
- lead pencil
- scissors and glue

Indications:

Skills, techniques, technologies and processes

- Uses a collage of photographs to inspire an artwork.
- Alters an image to combine many parts into a meaningful 'whole'.

Responding, reflecting on and evaluating visual arts

- Brings together a number of images to create a united concept for an artwork.
- Stretches reality to invent a new image.

Inspiration

- Students give examples of things that are real and things that are impossible or 'unreal'. For example, pigs are real, but pigs with wings are impossible or 'unreal'.
- Students imagine 'unreal' activities such as walking on air or swimming with a human body, but with fins for arms.
- Ask the students to look through magazines and allow their imaginations to 'run wild.'

Instructions

Step 1

The students will need to find several magazine cuttings prior to this activity. The cuttings should follow a particular theme or an idea the student may have.

Encourage students to think about the theme of their collage and how the cuttings should fit together to create a picture that combines 'real' objects in an 'unreal' or extreme way. When the students are happy with their design, they can glue the cuttings into place. Allow the students to add missing elements to their collage to help it make sense. In this style of drawing, the more 'unlikely' it is, the more interesting the final piece will be.

Step 2

Using lead pencil, copy the pictures in the collage onto a separate sheet of paper so they form one drawing. The students should feel free to alter the pictures in their cuttings to fit in with their new composition and make additions where necessary to help their picture make more sense.

Step 3

Colour the picture using felt-tipped pens or coloured pencils, or a combination of both. The students should blend the colours of one magazine image into another.

'Unreal' drawing

Step 4 Choose an 'unreal' colour – a colour that is in the drawing, but would not usually be associated with the subject matter chosen, to make a frame for the work. Display the artworks in an unusual place, such as pinned to the ceiling of the classroom.

Reflection questions

- What is 'unreal' about your drawing?
- Explain how you came up with the ideas for your drawing.
- Were you able to find many magazine pictures to help you with your design? Did you need to draw many additions for it to 'make sense'?
- How did you go about linking your pictures together to create your drawing?
- Are you pleased with the finished artwork?

Variations

- Make collages from magazine pictures to 'tell a story' or describe a situation.
- Cut large magazine pictures in half and draw the missing half.
- Draw a picture of an 'unreal' situation and glue on a photograph of their face or body as if they are participating in the activity.

Cross-curricular activities

- Read short stories from Paul Jennings books such as *Unreal* or *Unbelievable*.
- Invent an extreme sport. Draw diagrams detailing the sport and labelling its extreme features.
- Tell the students some unbelievable true stories about amazing survivals or escapes. Students write their own unbelievable survival or escape stories.

Resources

- pencil
- round object to trace/compass
- black fine-tipped pen
- ruler
- white paper
- black card for mounting
- scissors

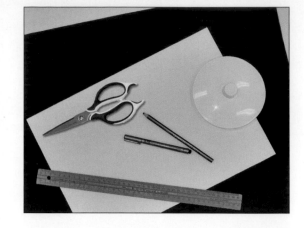

Indications:

Skills, techniques, technologies and processes

- Creates thick and thin lines to alter the appearance of distances.
- Measures accurately to achieve equidistant lines and create an optical illusion.

Responding, reflecting on and evaluating visual arts

- Looks at line drawings designed to 'trick' the eye and sees the image from a different perspective.
- Understands that in some drawings, precision is important.

Inspiration

- Look at pictures of optical illusions such as *Supernovae* by Vasarely (1961), or computer-generated images.
- Look at images that have a negative-positive silhouette.
- Investigate the way lines close together give a different illusion from lines further apart.
- Look for places in nature such as a field of swaying grass, where lines portray an image.

Instructions

Step 1

Trace around a large round object or use a compass to draw a circle of approximately 20 cm diameter. Find the centre of the circle. This can be done by folding the circle in opposite directions and marking the spot where the fold lines intersect.

Draw a faint line from edge to edge through the centre point of the circle. Draw a second line in the same way to create four quarters.

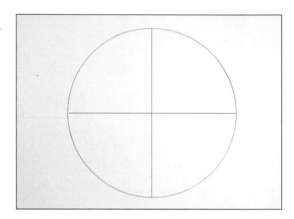

Step 2

Make small dots from the centre point along each line at 5 mm intervals.

Find the central point between each of the lines on the circumference of the circle. Again, these centre points can be found by folding and forming light creases.

Begin drawing lines from each of these centre points on the circumference to the dots at 5 mm intervals on the lines either side of it. Continue drawing the lines until each of the dots has been connected to a central dot. Encourage the students to check their work and to make any corrections.

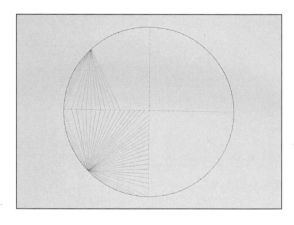

Step 3

Trace over each line carefully with a black fine-tipped pen. Cut around the circumference of the circle.

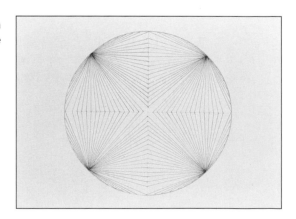

Optical illusion

Step 4

To add impact to the optical illusion, the students can add colour between some of the lines. This should be done sparingly to avoid affecting the illusion of depth created through the lines already drawn.

Reflection questions

- How does your optical illusion picture 'trick' the eye?
- Which areas look closer? Further away? What creates these effects?
- Did you measure carefully? Was it important to measure? Why do you think this?
- Are you happy with your artwork? Could you add to it in some way?

Variations

- Vary the thickness, colour and distance between the lines to alter the optical illusion.
- Experiment with other measured line patterns to create original optical illusions.
- Experiment with ways of creating 3-D objects from a 2-D drawing. Begin by drawing cubes on dot paper.

Cross-curricular activities

- Allow the students to share experiences when their eyes played 'tricks' on them.
- Investigate how mirrors can distort an image.
- Use lenses to refract and redirect light.
- Make simple 'flick' books to demonstrate how the eye can be tricked into thinking an object is moving.
- Hold a 'magic' afternoon, allowing the students to perform simple magic tricks or optical illusions.

Resources
- three shells
- strong glue
- pink, red and orange pencils
- lead pencil
- sand
- sand-coloured card
- red card for mounting

Indications:

Skills, techniques, technologies and processes

- Uses different pressures to create a variety of tones with one drawing implement.
- Draws shells from life.

Responding, reflecting on and evaluating visual arts

- Enjoys giving depth and perspective to flat shapes.
- Understands there can be many shades or tints of a single colour.

Inspiration

- Provide 2B, 4B and 6B pencils for the students to use and compare.
- Allow the students to experiment with the use of different pressures to create different shades.
- Use lead pencil to create a shaded strip ranging from white to dark grey.
- Look at the way shells have darker and lighter segments. Discuss possible reasons.

Instructions

Step 1

Ask the students to think about how they will fit the drawings of the three shells across the card so they will take up as much space as possible. Students draw an outline of each of the shells onto their card as planned. The students can then add segment lines to their shapes (a maximum of four for each shape).

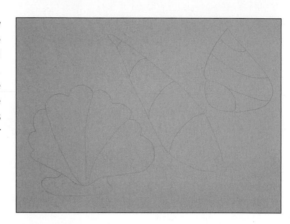

Step 2

Discuss how changing the pressure applied while colouring affects the colour produced; i.e. the heavier the colouring, the darker the colour. Challenge the students to colour each segment of one of their shells using a red pencil so each segment is progressively darker. Repeat this process for the other shells. Students may choose different colours for the other shells. The students should assess each segment they have coloured to ensure it is lighter or darker accordingly.

Step 3

Trace around each shell heavily in the chosen colour for that shell. Use strong glue to draw watermarks around the shells to give the illusion they are laying on a sandy beach. Sprinkle the glue with sand and allow the glue to dry.

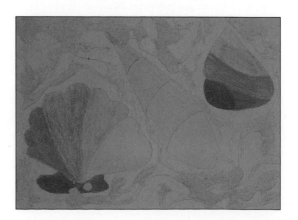

Shell shading

Step 4 Once the glue has dried thoroughly, mount the drawing onto red card. Alternatively, the drawings can be displayed en masse to create a sandy shoreline. For added effect, the students may like to glue small shells, fishing net or dried seaweed onto the drawings or display.

Reflection questions

- Were your shell drawings a good likeness to the shells?
- Does your colouring gradually become heavier in each section of the shell? Was this easy to do?
- How does using coloured pencils to create shading compare with using lead pencil?

Variations

- Make a shade cube. Draw a cube net and colour each of the squares in a different shade of a single colour.
- Draw three-dimensional shapes and use shading to enhance the 3-D effect.
- Add shadows to objects in drawings to give an illusion of dimension and perspective.

Cross-curricular activities

- Classify shells into molluscs or bivalves. Research other types of shells and start a class collection writing each shell's name and classification.
- Compare land snails to sea snails.
- Find out how pearls are cultivated and formed inside an oyster shell. Research the locations of today's pearl industry.
- Imagine being a pearl diver. Write an underwater adventure from the pearl diver's perspective.

Glossary – Drawing

bird's-eye view	view from overhead; for example, from a plane
closed shape	shape with a complete boundary
complementary colours	colours occurring on the opposite side of the colour wheel
composition	the putting together of parts to make a whole
distort	to twist out of shape
dominant	ruling, prevailing, or most influential element
etch	to cut or eat into a surface; for example, acid eating into metal
fauvism	an art movement that set out to heighten the emotional impact with exaggerated rich colours and unnatural forms
grip	way in which a tool is grasped while in use
landscape	(a) a painting of country scenery (b) horizontal layout of a rectangular page
linear pattern	a pattern formed in a line
medium	a means or material used by an artist to produce a work of art
mixed media	an artwork of which more than one type of medium has been used
mount	to fix on or in a position or setting
open shape	shape without a completed boundary, a line
optical illusion	involuntary mental misinterpretation of things seen due to its deceptive appearance
pastel	(a) a soft pale colour; (b) a soft, chalky crayon; (c) a drawing made with soft, chalky crayons
perspective	the appearance of distance as well height and width, produced on a flat surface
portrait	(a) a painting, drawing or photograph of someone, especially of his/her face; (b) rectangular paper placed vertically (as against landscape)
profile	an outline drawing of a face, especially a side view
radiating pattern	a pattern that spreads out like rays from a centre
refract	deflect light at a certain angle when it enters obliquely from another medium of different density
rotational pattern	a pattern formed by replicating objects in a circular rotation
still life	the depiction of lifeless things such as ornaments, fruit and musical instruments
tone	(a) the lightness or darkness of a colour; (b) general effect of colour or of light and shade in a picture
translucent	allowing some light to come through

Useful websites

Artist and art movements

National Gallery of Art	www.nga.gov
Time line of art history	www.metmuseum.org/toah/splash.htm
Australian Aboriginal Art	www.aboriginalartonline.com
Paul Cezanne	www.artchive.com/artchive/C/cezanne.html
Henri Matisse Art Gallery	www.geocities.com/Paris/LeftBank/4208/
Picasso	www.picasso.com/
Victor Vasarely	www.masterworksfineart.com/inventory/vasarely.htm

Art Education

The incredible art department	www.princetonol.com/groups/iad/
Magical places and creative spaces	www.allthedaze.com
Picasso	www.surfnetkids.com/picasso.htm

Tools and techniques

Terminology and art index	www.artlex.com

Painting

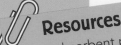

Resources
- absorbent paper towels
- food colouring/edicol dye
- black marking pen
- newspaper
- red and green card for mounting

Indications:

Skills, techniques, technologies and processes

- Uses a dropper to apply appropriate amounts of dye to a surface.
- Understands that when colours mix they create new colours.

Responding, reflecting on and evaluating visual arts

- Visualizes and marks outlines using irregular shapes as boundaries and guides.
- Uses imagination to transform an irregular pattern into a picture.

Inspiration

- Give the students ample opportunity to explore how dye spreads on absorbent paper towel.
- Direct the students to mix colours by allowing them to 'bleed' into each other.
- Look at places in nature where camouflage occurs.
- Discuss how chameleons can change colour to suit their surroundings.

Instructions

Step 1

Place several sheets of newspaper on the work area. Ensure all students are wearing protective clothing through which dye cannot be absorbed. Plastic painting smocks are ideal. Place a sheet of thick, absorbent paper towel on the newspaper. Use food colouring or brightly coloured edicol dye. Place several drops on one spot on the paper towel. Watch the dye spread and become absorbed into the towel.

Step 2

Use the same colour dye in several other places on the paper and watch them spread and absorb. Select another colour and repeat the process. It is best to apply colours from the lightest to the darkest. As the colours come into contact with one another, they will mix to create new colours. When using darker colours, add drops slowly to ensure they do not overtake the lighter colours completely. Allow the paper to dry. Do not attempt to lift the paper towel from the newspaper until it is completely dry.

Step 3

Look at the shapes created by the mixed colours. Encourage the students to use their imagination to see 'bug creatures' in the blob pattern. Use the example of looking for objects or animals in the clouds to help the students visualise imaginary bugs. Use a black marking pen to outline colour shapes to create body segments, wings, legs and a head 'camouflaged' among the colours on the paper towel.

Camouflage bugs

Step 4

Mount the 'camouflage bug' against strong colours. Alternatively, the bugs can also be combined into one large camouflage mural where all of the students' bugs can be discovered within a strikingly colourful display.

Reflection questions

- Did the dye create the colours you expected when they bled together?
- Were you happy with the bug you 'discovered' in the picture?
- What part of the process did you enjoy most?
- Do you think the dye would behave differently on a different surface?

Variations

- Experiment with dye on other less absorbent papers.
- Allow the students to use fine paintbrushes with dye at full strength and dye at diluted strengths to paint a simple 'watercolour'.
- For a similar effect, students draw on wet paper with felt-tipped pens. Allow the paper to dry before adding fine details.

Cross-curricular activities

- Discover why some creatures camouflage themselves.
- Play hide and seek. Discuss why we might feel the need to hide sometimes.
- Brainstorm to make a list of scary things and use them as a stimulus for scary 'hiding' stories.

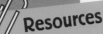
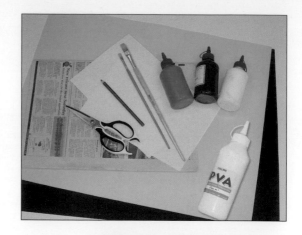

Resources

- black, orange and white paint
- newspaper
- white paper
- thick and thin paintbrushes
- pencil
- green and black card for mounting
- ruler (optional)
- scissors and strong glue

Indications:

Skills, techniques, technologies and processes

- Uses techniques consistent with pop art to reproduce that style.

Responding, reflecting on and evaluating visual arts

- Recognises the features of pop art.
- Applies the characteristics of pop art to design and create their own pop art painting.

Inspiration

- Look at artworks by Roy Lichtenstein and Andy Warhol. Discuss the techniques used, the colours chosen and the effect achieved.
- Discuss where the students might have seen pop art before.
- Look at a colour wheel and discuss colours that look bold against each other or are 'complementary'.

Instructions

Step 1

Use a thick paintbrush to paint a sheet of art paper black. The black surface should be 'flat' with no irregularities such as lighter or darker areas. Alternatively, the students could be provided with black paper or card to work on. Dip the end of a pencil in white paint to print white dots, evenly spaced in a regular array pattern over the surface. The dots can be as far apart or as close together as desired, so long as they are all equidistant. It may help to use a ruler and mark the places where the dots need to go, prior to printing.

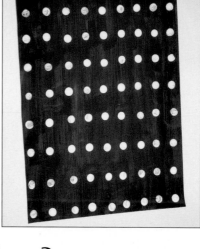

Step 2

Show the students some examples of pop art if they have not already seen some. Note that many include a cartoon-like character and a speech bubble. The students should be encouraged to be as imaginative as possible when creating their character. Suggest the students think beyond human characters, and imagine talking animals or even plants and what they might say. On a separate sheet of paper, draw the cartoon figure. Use one bright colour only and black detail to paint the character. When it is dry, cut around the shape.

Step 3

Draw a speech bubble that will fit onto the pre-prepared dotted sheet with the cartoon character. Inside the speech bubble, write a message for the character to say in pencil. Carefully paint the boundary of the speech bubble and the lettering in black paint with a thin round paintbrush. Cut out the speech bubble when it is dry.

Pop art

Step 4

Glue the character and its speech bubble to the black and white background. Mount against a vibrant colour that contrasts with the colour of the character.

Reflection questions

- Did I choose colours that stand out and give the picture a bold appearance?
- Does my artwork look like pop art? What could I have done to make it more in keeping with that style?
- What were the more difficult/easier aspects of the task?

Variations

- Encourage the students to explore a range of colour combinations beyond simple black and white and one contrasting colour.
- Students paint a self-portrait with a speech bubble, making comment about a school issue or advertising for an upcoming school event.
- Students use a computer-generated pattern as a background for their artwork or attempt to create the complete picture using drawing software and an everyday subject matter.

Cross-curricular activities

- Allow the students to browse through advertising catalogues. Discuss the way colours, words and layout are used to attract attention. Discuss what stands out the most.
- Investigate goods and services provided in the local community.
- Observe the old-fashioned style of the characters used in pop art. Investigate what life might have been like living at that time and how it would be different to our lifestyle today.

Resources

- red and brown edicol dye
- thick paintbrushes
- white paper
- red paper square
- newspaper
- black card for mounting
- scissors and glue
- black paint
- water
- drinking straw

Indications:

Skills, techniques, technologies and processes

- Directs dye across a page by blowing through a straw.

Responding, reflecting on and evaluating visual arts

- Assesses where to direct dye in order to produce a balanced image.
- Adds dye to an image where needed to create a more realistic 'campfire' effect.

Inspiration

- Light a candle and observe how a flame moves and changes. Blow on it lightly to watch the flame flicker. Note the transparent colour of the flame.
- Look at pictures of fires.
- Students close their eyes and imagine they are sitting around a campfire. Discuss how it looks, sounds and smells.

Instructions

Step 1

Place a sheet of art paper in a portrait position over several layers of newspaper. Ensure the students are wearing suitable protective clothing through which dye cannot seep. Plastic painting smocks are ideal.

Use a thick black paintbrush and black paint to paint a series of 'logs'. These logs will become the base of the campfire and can be built up in several brushstrokes into a 'tepee' shape. Allow the paint to dry.

Step 2

Prepare solutions of bright red and brown edicol dye. Dip a straw into the dye. Place a thumb over the end of the straw to seal it and create a vacuum. Lift the straw into a position over the 'campfire' logs and release the seal, releasing the dye onto the page. Repeat this process and create several blobs of red and brown dye on the logs.

Step 3

Use the straws as a funnel through which to channel air to blow the dye blobs in random directions across the page and create 'flames'. Attempt to blow the flames so that they spread up the page as real flames would. Where necessary, add dye to the page to 'thicken' up areas at the base of the flames. Set the painting aside and allow it to dry. This may take some time.

Campfire

Step 4

Cut around the flames and the campfire logs. Glue the campfire onto red coloured paper square cut into a simple flame shape and mount on a black background. The white internal shapes can be left 'white hot', coloured in charcoal or in bright yellows and oranges.

Reflection questions

- Was it easy to control the edicol dye using a straw to blow it?
- Do you think your flames look realistic? Do they give the effect of fire?
- How would you describe the feelings your painting gives the viewer?
- How else could you have mounted your painting?

Variations

- Using the same technique with green and brown dye, blow it horizontally across the page to create spiky bramble bushes.
- Put a large blob of black dye into the centre of a page and blow outwards using a straw to create a spider's web. Use a black fine-tipped pen to add finer web lines.

Cross-curricular activities

- Investigate native animals and how they shelter themselves in the wild. Find out about protection they may have against fires.
- Conduct an overnight camping trip where the students are given an opportunity to observe an open campfire.
- Construct a list of requirements for a camping trip.
- Develop a campfire menu and hold a barbecue to try an item on the menu.

- newspaper
- green, blue, white and black paint in squirt bottles
- several sheets white paper
- green and black card for mounting
- straight-edged object
- objects to use for drawing e.g. comb, toothbrush, paintbrush
- glass

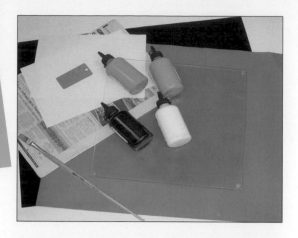

Indications:

Skills, techniques, technologies and processes

- Uses a straight-edged object to spread and mix paint over a printing surface.
- Takes a print from a painted surface.
- Uses everyday objects as tools for making pictorial impressions in wet paint.

Responding, reflecting on and evaluating visual arts

- Understands how black print over blue and green print is symbolic of pollution.
- Makes several prints and chooses the most successful to display.

Inspiration

- Brainstorm a list of things that pollute our environment.
- Use a picture of a natural environment as a background. Students glue 'pollutants' made from materials used in collages to demonstrate how pollution changes an environment.
- Students run their fingers over a dirty surface in the playground such as play equipment or bench seats and note the dirt or 'pollution' evident there. (Ensure the students wash their hands thoroughly afterwards).

Instructions

Step 1

Prepare a sheet of glass, plastic or other smooth surface by cleaning and removing any residue. Place several sheets of newspaper on a flat surface in readiness for the prints to be made. Organise several sheets of white paper for printing.

Squirt lines of green, blue and white paint across the printing surface.

Step 2

Use a straight-edged tool to spread and smooth the paint across the printing surface. The colours should be mixed slightly but not blended completely. When the consistency of paint across the printing surface is relatively even, take a sheet of white paper and place it over the painted area. Press evenly, but not too firmly across the surface of the paper. Lift the paper from the print surface carefully so as not to smudge the printed paper. Place the prints on newspaper to dry. Take a second and third print from the same print surface. The prints will become progressively lighter each time. Repeat the process if desired. Allow all the prints to dry. Clean the print surface thoroughly, removing all traces of paint.

Step 3

Squirt black paint onto the cleaned print surface and spread evenly with a straight-edged tool. Use everyday objects such as the end of a paintbrush, a comb or a toothbrush to etch a picture into the wet paint of a city scene with pollution coming out of cars and buildings. Press onto a sheet of the previously printed green and blue paper to reveal a polluted cityscape. Take several prints and redraw the picture if necessary to make clean prints. *Note: Too much paint will cause the prints to smudge and the image will be lost.*

Polluted city

Step 4   Allow the prints to dry and select the print which gives the best image of pollution overtaking a natural landscape. Mount on green and black card.

Reflection questions

- How did you spread the paint on the glass or plastic surface? What did it feel like?
- How did the paint change when it was transferred onto the paper?
- Did you like your picture better before or after the second print?
- What difficulties did you encounter during the printing process?
- Did your final picture give the desired effect?

Variations

- Draw onto the first layer of paint for a single layer print.
- Use different tools to create unusual patterns in the paint on the glass surface. Mix colours on the glass surface using these utensils or fingers.
- Use a patterned 'lift-off' print as a background for other painted artworks or artworks created with materials used in collages.

Cross-curricular activities

- Investigate the ways we pollute our environment and how we could reduce pollution.
- Compare what is in the local environment now to what would have been there 200 years ago. How has it changed?
- Write stories from the perspective of frogs whose environments are threatened.
- Become involved in a recycling project.

Resources
- purple, blue, green and white paint
- paintbrushes of different thicknesses
- white paper
- aqua and light coloured card for mounting
- palette; e.g. lid of an ice-cream container
- newspaper
- scissors and glue

Indications:

Skills, techniques, technologies and processes

- Controls paintbrushes of different sizes and shapes to produce a desired image.
- Uses contrasting lines, colours and patterns.

Responding, reflecting on and evaluating visual arts

- Observes pictures of a giant clam and attempts to recreate them using line and colour.
- Copies and invents patterns to describe patterns occurring in nature.

Inspiration

- Students use a variety of implements to create different paint effects and patterns.
- Allow the students to pool their ideas and copy the techniques of others.
- Look at photos of giant clams. Note the colours and concentric nature of the patterns.
- Find out how big giant clams can grow. Mark on outline in chalk on the ground to show the students.

Instructions
Step 1

Look at pictures of living open clams. Observe the wavy shape of the 'mouth' and the colours and patterning. On a large sheet of art paper, draw a single wavy line in green using a thick paintbrush. Use the line as the centre guideline for your clam.

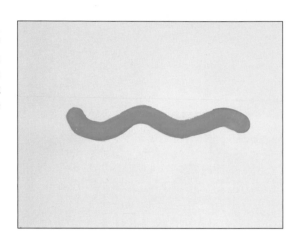

Step 2

Use a palette on which to put blue, green and purple paint. Using only these colours, mix combinations to create new colours. Paint some concentric lines around the green guide line in plain blue or purple and others in the newly created colours. The aim should be to paint lines that become progressively darker from the inside to the outside. These lines should also be painted using a thick paintbrush. Allow to dry.

Step 3

Using narrower flat and round brushes, and only plain blue, green and purple paint, add detailed patterns. Each of the concentric lines should have its own unique pattern. That pattern should be painted in a colour that will stand out against the line it is painted on. Using a fine round paintbrush, paint a single line in purple along the centre of the green central guideline.

Giant clam

Step 4 Cut around the clam shape. Trace a shape slightly wider than the clam onto light-coloured card to become the shell and cut out this shape also. Mount onto an aqua background. Add to the display with tropical fish, coral created from brightly coloured polystyrene balls and seaweed made from strips of green garbage bags.

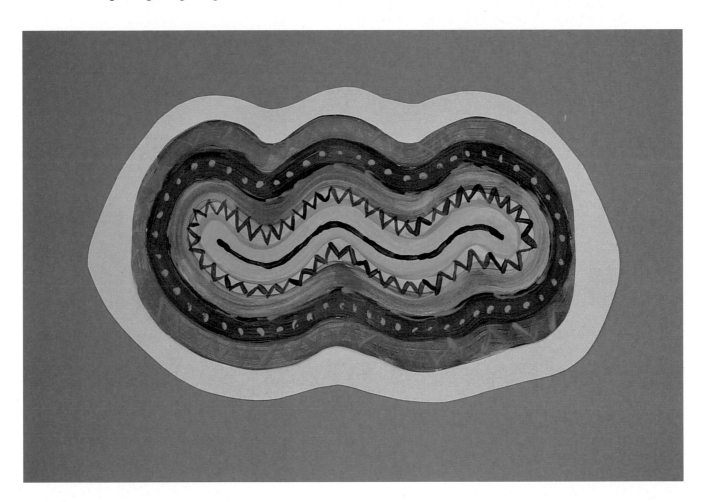

Reflection questions

- What tools or techniques made the best patterns?
- Do you think it is more important to make a clam in your artwork look realistic or attractive?
- How many different greens did you mix? Could you have mixed more? What other colours could you have added to green to change the colour?

Variations

- Students create patterned wrapping paper using one or two different patterns.
- Encourage the students to experiment with dragging tools such as a comb or toothbrush across a wet paint surface.
- Explore patterns using flowing lines or shapes or jagged lines or shapes, or combine two or three colours in a sequence to create a pattern.

Cross-curricular activities

- Investigate creatures that live in coral reefs.
- Investigate different types of shells, in particular, bivalves, such as clams and oysters. Discuss how pearls are formed.
- Trace around cockle shells onto grid paper and calculate their area and perimeter.
- Conduct an excursion to the beach. Collect shells for classification and observe creatures living in rock pools.

Resources

- green, purple and orange paint
- fine-tipped paintbrush
- pencil
- newspaper
- green and purple card for mounting
- two sheets of white paper
- thick paintbrush
- glue

Indications:

Skills, techniques, technologies and processes

- Uses a combination of secondary colours to create art.
- Draws and paints an object realistically.

Responding, reflecting on and evaluating visual arts

- Understands that secondary colours are mixed from primary colours.

Inspiration

- Look at the colour wheel. Identify the primary colours (yellow, blue, red) and the colours which are created when two are mixed. (green, orange and purple).
- Students mix pairs of primary colours to make secondary colours and complete a colour wheel of their own. (See Step 1.)
- Students obtain a piece of fruit to be a still life model for drawing and painting elements of the artwork.

Instructions

Step 1

Review secondary colours – colours that occur when primary colours (red, yellow and blue) are mixed. This can best be demonstrated by painting colour wheels. Students draw a circle and divide it into six equal segments. Paint three of the segments in yellow, blue and red leaving a blank section between each. The students can then combine red and yellow paint to make orange and paint the section between red and yellow in orange. Repeat this process for blue and yellow to make green, and blue and red to make purple to complete the colour wheel. Identify the three secondary colours (orange, purple and green). Ask the students to think of a fruit or vegetable that is a secondary colour and select one of these to be their subject. Use a different secondary colour to paint a sheet of paper.

Step 2

On a second sheet of paper, draw a simplified outline of the subject in pencil.

Step 3

Paint the subject in its appropriate secondary colour. When dry, use the third remaining secondary colour to paint detail onto the subject using a fine-tipped paintbrush.

Secondary colours

Step 4 When the painting is dry, glue the subject onto the painted background sheet. Mount against a secondary colour.

Reflection questions

- How do the secondary colours look together in your finished artwork?
- Does your still life painting look realistic? How could it be improved?
- What other things would have made a good still life subject for your picture?

Variations

- Use backgrounds of a secondary colour as stimulus for an artwork. For example; a green grasshopper on an orange, or a purple lily on a green lily pad.
- Use secondary colours as an alternative to true colours. For example, a purple sky with orange grass and green sun. Encourage the students to think laterally about their colour choices.

Cross-curricular activities

- Classify foods into food groups and discuss healthy food choices.
- Make fruit salad to share.
- Look at other ways we can keep our bodies healthy such as keeping clean and exercising.
- Conduct a survey of snacks eaten by students in the class.
- Cut fruit to create a variety of different cross-sections.

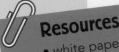

Resources
- white paper
- all paint colours except white
- black marking pen
- thin and thick paintbrushes
- blue and yellow card for mounting
- newspaper
- glue

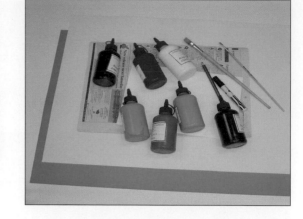

Indications:

Skills, techniques, technologies and processes

- Controls a paint brush to paint within a given boundary.
- Works within given parameters to produce original work.

Responding, reflecting on and evaluating visual arts

- Identifies similarities and differences between their own artwork and other examples of modern art.
- Assesses and adjusts own work to create a balanced image.

Inspiration

- Look at examples of modern art. Discuss the distinctive features of this style of painting.
- Observe how a colour is enhanced when put against a black background.
- Make black 'frames' to enhance colours around the room.

Instructions

Step 1

Show the students examples of modern art. Discuss the simplicity of the lines and shapes used and the boldness and contrast of the colours.

Students draw five shapes onto a blank sheet of art paper. Each shape should be a different size, and be flowing. Encourage the students to use as much of the page as possible and to overlap shapes, in their drawing.

Step 2

Paint each of the shapes in either a bold primary or secondary colour. Where the shapes overlap, the newly created shape should be painted in contrasting colour. The students should be encouraged to plan, visualise and assess their colour choices prior to painting. Allow to dry.

Step 3

Use a thin, flat paintbrush to paint the area surrounding the painted shapes in black. This will make the colours appear more vibrant.

Modern art

Step 4 Use a black marking pen to retrace internal lines and make the colours more pronounced. Mount on vibrant-coloured card. The colours should match those in the painting.

Variations

- Create closed shapes made up of only vertical and horizontal lines rather than flowing 'organic' shapes.
- Cut around the outline of the combined shapes and mount on coloured paper.
- Draw a series of symmetrical overlapping shapes. Use only two colours to paint a negative/positive image.

Reflection questions

- Why did you choose to put each colour where you did?
- What makes the colours stand out so boldly?
- Why do you think your artwork looks modern?
- What words would you use to describe the shapes you drew?

Cross-curricular activities

- Compare modern art to art from the 16th and 17th centuries. Discuss how and why you think they have changed.
- Draw a time line of the last 2 000 years, including major events.
- Draw the students' attention to the way we refer to different centuries. For example, the 18th century is the 1700s.
- Introduce or revise Roman numerals to describe large numbers.

Resources

- black paper
- aluminium foil
- toothpicks
- yellow and white paint
- silver or metallic card for mounting
- gold and silver glitter (optional)
- spare paper for experimentation
- fine paintbrushes
- scissors and glue

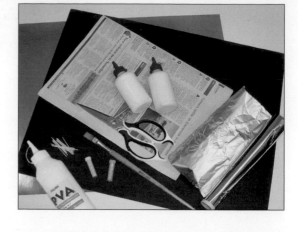

Indications:

Skills, techniques, technologies and processes

- Uses a toothpick to direct paint into desired shapes.
- Randomly positions 'stars' across a page so they appear unplanned, but are evenly distributed.

Responding, reflecting on and evaluating visual arts

- Enjoys exploring new techniques.

Inspiration

- Observe shiny objects such as aluminium foil or mirrors in the sunlight. Students squint their eyes to look at strong lights to distort them. Discuss how they distort by blurring and creating radiating lines from the light source.
- Look at traditional star shapes.
- Look at the night sky and squint to distort the stars.

Instructions

Step 1

Place several blobs of yellow paint randomly over a black paper square. Make smaller blobs of white paint scattered among the yellow blobs and also on top of the yellow blobs. The aim should be to create a night sky where the stars are randomly positioned – not following a set pattern. At the same time, the stars should be spread so they are not all clumped in one area. Emphasise the need to balance the spread of stars without arranging them in a regular pattern.

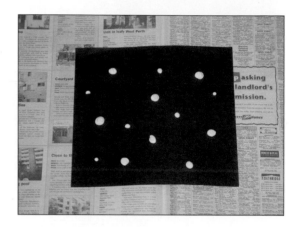

Step 2

On a separate sheet of paper, experiment with paint blobs using a toothpick to drag the paint and create star shapes. Once satisfied with the technique developed, apply it to the paint blobs on the black paper square. Some stars should be bigger or 'brighter' than others in the same way they would in a night sky.

Step 3

Fold small squares of foil in half four times and press firmly. Use a marking pen to draw a small star onto the foil. Cut out the small star shape. Separate the foil to produce several stars. Repeat this process to create the stars required to add to the star painting.

Splatter stars

Step 4

Attach the stars to the 'night sky' scene. Use a fine paintbrush to add small white spots among the splatter stars to create stars in the distance. Sprinkle glitter, if desired, on the 'distant stars' while they are still wet. Mount on a silver or metallic background.

Reflection questions

- Why was it easier to use the end of a paintbrush rather that the brush itself for making the distant stars?
- Did you incorporate any special constellations into your painting?
- Could you have done anything differently to enhance your painting?

Variations

- Use the same technique to make iridescent plankton using fluorescent paint on dark blue card. Include radiating jellyfish-style tentacles.
- Make balloons by dragging string lines from brightly coloured paint blobs. Spread the remaining blobs to create larger balloons using the brush end of a paintbrush.

Cross-curricular activities

- Use constellation maps to identify notable stars, constellations and the Milky Way. Investigate the planets and their moons.
- Construct models of space transportation using folded, rolled or torn paper to create a three-dimensional shape.
- Use dot paper to construct drawings of shapes with a specified number of sides (including star shapes.)

Resources
• white paper
• newspaper
• water
• paintbrushes
• blue, green, yellow and red powder paint
• orange card for mounting

Indications:

Skills, techniques, technologies and processes

• Experiments with dry paint particles on a wet surface.

• Uses a paintbrush to direct and blend the flow of paint on a wet surface to create a desired look.

Responding, reflecting on and evaluating visual arts

• Assesses whether they have created the impression of a landscape using a new technique.

• Identifies areas that could be treated differently or improved in future experiences with the new technique.

Inspiration

• Look at pictures of barren 'outback' land. Note the strength and contrast of colour.

• Look at artwork depicting an outback colour scheme.

• Experiment with powder paint on large sheets of wet butcher's paper to develop an understanding of how the paint and water combine to create strong colours.

Instructions

Step 1

Prepare a large area with newspaper. Do not use protective plastic sheeting, as it is important that excess liquid has something to soak into. This will prevent the picture from becoming too sodden and unmanageable.

Wet half a sheet of white art paper with a sponge or by dipping it into water. The paper will need to be quite wet for the powder paint to liquefy.

Step 2

Sprinkle blue powder paint randomly across the wet section of the paper. Use a paintbrush to move the powder around and help it to form paint. Do not overwork the particles, allowing some to remain relatively intact. Use the brush to add additional water to the page if necessary, to assist the paint to flow into unusual sky patterns. When satisfied, allow the sky section to dry on a flat surface. This may take some time.

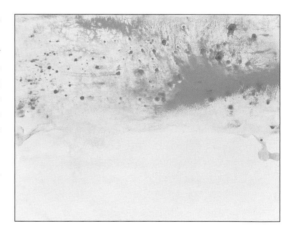

Step 3

When dry, repeat the process, wetting the opposite side of the paper completely and sprinkling yellow and red powder paint onto the wet surface. Again, use a paintbrush to move the particles around, dissolving them and mixing the colours slightly to create vivid oranges and a barren landscape. Add water with a paintbrush to assist movement of the particles if required. Allow the painting to dry on a flat surface.

Watercolour landscape

Step 4   When dry, use a paintbrush to apply water in small patches to the bottom half of the paper. Sprinkle green powder paint on these areas but do not mix them. Allow them to sit and dry in particle form to create sparse vegetation on the desert landscape. Mount on an orange background.

Reflection questions

- What happened to the powder paint when it came in contact with the paper?
- Were you able to control the flow of the watery paint the way you wanted to?
- Describe how you mixed the yellow and red powder paint. Did you get the colour you were hoping for?
- Were you happy with your image once it had dried? What could you do to add 'character' to your desert scene?

Variations

- Wet a sheet of art paper completely. Sprinkle with salt and powder paint and spread gently with additional water. Allow it to dry, creating a 'silk painting' on paper.
- Create appropriate watercolour backgrounds for painting, printing or collage work.
- Cut out shapes from 'watercoloured' paper to add to displays.

Cross-curricular activities

- Make paper pulp and recycle to use as paper. Add different scents to the developing paper and press flowers and ferns into the paper as it sets.
- Conduct an experiment to investigate the absorbency of different types of paper.
- Experiment with different liquids to discover which will float on, mix with or sink in water.
- Fill a glass jar with water and add a thin layer of vegetable oil. Drop food colouring on the surface and gently break the surface tension so small rainbow ribbons of dye fall through the water.

Resources

- fine paintbrush
- pencil
- red card for mounting
- straight-edged object
- black marking pen
- orange, red, yellow, purple and white paint in squirt bottles
- black paint
- newspaper
- white paper

Indications:

Skills, techniques, technologies and processes

- Uses a flat-edged tool to mix paint on canvas.
- Carefully paints intricate details to create a descriptive horizon.

Responding, reflecting on and evaluating visual arts

- Determines whether a desired horizon line has been achieved.
- Adds detail to a horizon to create a particular style or culture.

Inspiration

- Investigate how silhouettes are created. Where does the light come from?
- Brainstorm to list situations where silhouettes might occur. What are the potential light sources?
- Discuss how a particular outline or event can be described through shape only. Students suggest shapes that could be used to describe a Chinese festival, a tropical island or a night sky.

Instructions

Step 1

Prepare an area with newspaper or protective sheeting. Squirt strips of 'sunset' colours, including purple, red, yellow and white onto the top two thirds of a sheet of art paper. The colours should be the darkest at the top of the page to the lightest at the bottom of the section. Use a straight-edged tool to spread and mix the paint across the page, creating a sunset sky image. Do not mix the colours too much.

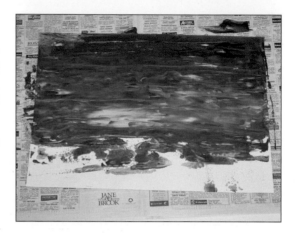

Step 2

Decide upon a particular landscape or scene you would like to represent through your horizon. Plan your horizon on a separate sheet of paper, in lead pencil first. Make additions or corrections where necessary and then transfer or redraw the finished horizon line in lead pencil onto the bottom of the sunset sky, approximately two thirds of the way down the page. Trace the line with a black marking pen.

Step 3

Use full strength black paint to paint the area below the horizon line. When dry, add small details with a black marking pen or fine paintbrush if required.

Sunset silhouette

Step 4   When dry, choose a colour from the sunset sky as a background to mount the finished painting onto. This activity looks particularly effective when paintings are displayed side by side, with horizons matching together to create a wide horizon of artworks representing different cultures or scenes.

Reflection questions

- What did you use as your spreading tool to create the sunset? Was it an effective tool?
- Did you enjoy the process of creating the sunset? Did the colours mix as expected? Did the finished painting look like a sunset?
- What landscape or scene did you make into a silhouette? What shapes did you use to portray this type of landscape or scene?

Variations

- Cut shapes or images from black paper and glue them onto a painted background to create a silhouette.
- Use dark coloured silhouettes (not necessarily black) to create a background for a picture. For example, a purple mountain range.
- Paint 'night' creatures as silhouettes in front of a huge silvery white moon.

Cross-curricular activities

- Make shadow puppets and use them to retell a familiar story.
- Identify different light sources and where the energy comes from to create these lights.
- Compare the lengths of a student's shadow at different times of day. Draw chalk lines and record a time for each.
- Make simple sundials and attempt to use them to work out the time of day.

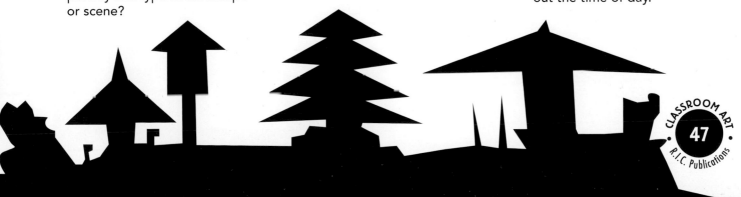

Resources

- black and white paint
- pencil
- picture or photocopy of a textured object to copy
- white paper
- newspaper
- black card for mounting
- glue

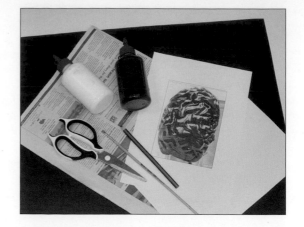

Indications:

Skills, techniques, technologies and processes

- Determines the appropriate lines to trace on an image with dark and light shading.
- Paints in layers from the lightest to the darkest colour.

Responding, reflecting on and evaluating visual arts

- Uses shapes, line and colour and their proximity to one another to assist in reproducing an image.
- Recognises when their own image differs from the original and attempts to correct it.

Inspiration

- Consolidate what is meant by 'texture'. Provide examples of many different textures for the students to view.
- Discuss what we can see that tells us without touching, that a surface is not flat .
- Shine a torch on a capsicum to illustrate how shadows reveal the texture and shape of an object that is a single colour.

Instructions

Step 1

Look through magazines or on the Internet for pictures of heavily-textured objects. Foods such as prunes work well. Choose a subject to attempt to copy using paints. If using a magazine picture, copy in black and white to assist you in seeing the dark and light areas of the texture. Similarly, a picture from an Internet site could be printed in black ink only. Draw the outline of the subject and draw in some of the more distinct dark and light areas in lead pencil.

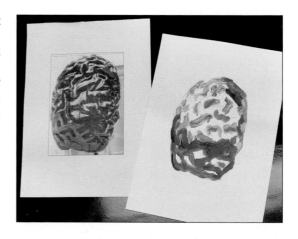

Step 2

In this activity you will need to paint layers of colour from light to dark, gradually adding more and more black to build up to the darkest colours. Begin by painting in white areas. Allow the paint to dry. Look carefully at the subject you are copying and add the lightest grey areas.

Step 3

Gradually add increasingly darker areas to the painting, allowing it to dry in between each layer. The final layer should be black.

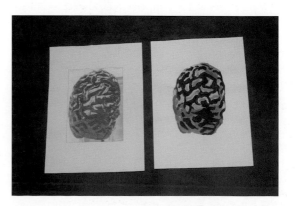

Painting texture

Step 4 When dry, cut around the subject shape and mount it onto black card. If desired, mount the original photocopied or printed subject next to it as a comparison for the viewer.

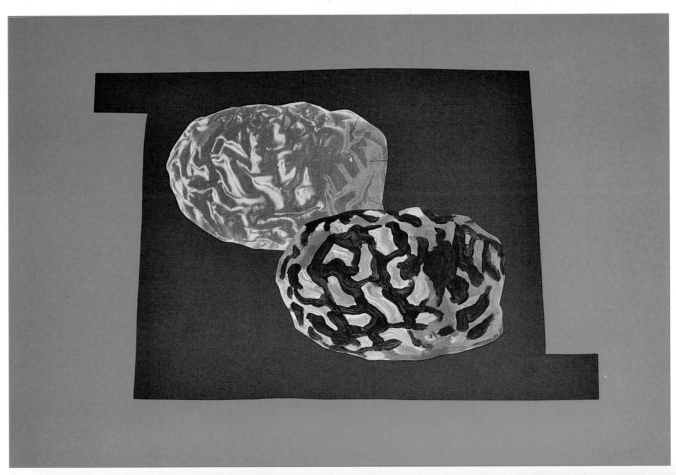

Reflection questions

- Did you trace or draw your image? Why did you choose to produce the image that way?
- What colour did you paint first? Why is this the most logical starting colour?
- Did you give your shape a textured look? How did you create this illusion?
- Does your painting look like the picture you copied? How are they alike or different? Are the differences important?

Variations

- Attempt to paint an image from still life using shadows to portray texture and shape. Suitable subjects include a hand or foot, ears, capsicums, pineapples, organic sculptures and seed pods.
- Draw a prism and paint different shades of a colour on each surface to create depth.
- Draw a coiled snake and paint in shadows along the body to make the body look round and to bring the snake to 'life'.

Cross-curricular activities

- Invent percussion instruments based on brushing or rubbing a textured surface.
- Investigate the body coverings of different animals. Determine why they need that type of covering to survive in their environment.
- Make a class cactus garden and note the way cactus leaves have adapted to suit it's environment.
- Write descriptions of walking over an unusual texture. How did it look, feel and sound?

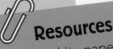

Resources

- white paper
- lead pencil
- blue, green, black and white paint
- paintbrush
- newspaper
- dark blue or green card for mounting

Indications:

Skills, techniques, technologies and processes

- Draws lines to represent the topography of an imagined stretch of land.
- Mixes shades and tints of a colour.

Responding, reflecting on and evaluating visual arts

- Identifies when a shade or tint is not distinct enough from the previous colour used.
- Appreciates that increasing depth of colour can indicate distance and dimension.

Inspiration

- Look at topographic maps in an atlas. Note the way the lines flow concentrically around each other. Discuss the heights these lines represent.
- Provide the students with long strips of paper and have them paint the strip, changing from one colour to another.

Instructions

Step 1

Look at the linear patterns on topographic maps. Read the maps to determine high and low sections of the map. Attempt to visualise what the landscape might look like. On a sheet of white art paper, use pencil to draw a series of concentric lines to create the mountains and valley on an imagined topographic map. Visualise what the map you have drawn would look like as a landscape.

Step 2

To give the 'map' depth, you will need to paint the highest point in the lightest colour and the lowest in the darkest colour. Choose a colour for your landscape. For example, an alpine landscape might have white snow caps and lush green hills, where a desert landscape might use tints and shades of orange or red. Locate the highest sections of your map and paint them in the lightest tint of the colour you have chosen. If they are to represent snow-capped mountains, the first colour may even be white. Gradually add more and more of your chosen colour to white to create increasingly darker colours. Paint each topographic 'ring' in a slightly darker colour as you progress down the mountain.

Step 3

To create the deep valleys on the map, add increasing amounts of black paint to the base colour for each topographic ring. If there is a stream as the base, you may choose to add increasing amounts of blue to the base colour as you descend.

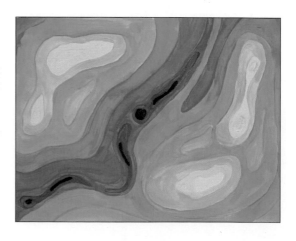

Mountains high and rivers deep

Step 4 When dry, mount the artwork on blue or green card. These paintings also look effective mounted side by side with similar paintings, to create a large topographic map. Students imagine and draw the horizon between different points of the display.

Variations

- Investigate how colour keys are used to describe information on different types of maps. Create a key and paint different kinds of maps accordingly.

- Use colour gradation to portray contours on prisms and spheres to give them a three-dimensional appearance.

- Practise creating gradients from one colour to another or across several colours to create a rainbow effect.

Cross-curricular activities

- Investigate what topographic maps describe. Use line graphs to draw the 'shape' of land on a section of a topographic map.

- Locate and mark important cities and landmarks on a map of a particular country.

- Look at a map of the local community. Identify the school, local streets where the students live, and community facilities.

- Students draw their own map of the school and plot the route for a one-kilometre run. Use a trundle wheel to check the distance and alter the course if necessary.

Reflection questions

- What landscape did you portray with your topographic map?
- What colour did you use for the highest points? What colour did you use for the lowest points? Why did you choose these colours?
- Describe how you changed one colour into another from the highest to the lowest points of the map.
- Are you happy with the colour gradient you created?

Glossary – Painting

balance achieved when similar or dissimilar elements compensate each other so adequately, that the result is perfect equilibrium

base colour a predominant starting colour to which other colours are added to create another colour or tone

camouflage a kind of disguise, either natural or human-made, that makes something hard to see among its surroundings

canvas heavy cotton cloth used for painting on, usually stretched across a wooden frame

colour gradient the gradual progression of one colour to another

concentric having the same centre; e.g. when a stone is dropped into water, the ripples form concentric circles

diluted made thinner or weaker by adding water

distort to twist out of shape

edicol dye created from natural products, often in the form of powder

lift-off prints placing paper over a painted surface and lifting away to create a print

modern art art from the 1860s to 1970s; includes periods such as impressionism, cubism, fauvism, expessionism, and futurism

organic having to do with living things or their organs

parametres guidelines with set boundaries in which to problem-solve and create

pop art an art movement using mass media subjects to draw attention to the apparent importance of commercialism

secondary colour colours produced when two base colours are mixed; e.g. red and yellow mix to create the secondary colour orange

shade to create a darker or lighter version of one colour

silhouette an outline drawing filled with black like a shadow

symbolism conveying an artistic message by means of associated ideas

tint a variety of colour made lighter by adding white

topography mapping of the surface of the land with reference to elevation

transparent easily seen through

watercolour paint made of pigment diluted with water and not oil; a painting done in watercolour

Useful websites

Artist and art movements

Art Museum network — www.amn.org
The Metropolitan Museum of Art — www.metmuseum.org
Art in context — www.artincontext.org/index.htm
Pop art — www.popartists.com/
Australian landscapes — amol.org.au/discovenet/tales/landscape.asp

Tools and techniques

Watercolour tips — website.lineone.net/~peter.saw/tips.html

Art education

Art junction — www.artjunction.org
Art education and ArtEdventures — www.alifetimeofcolor.com

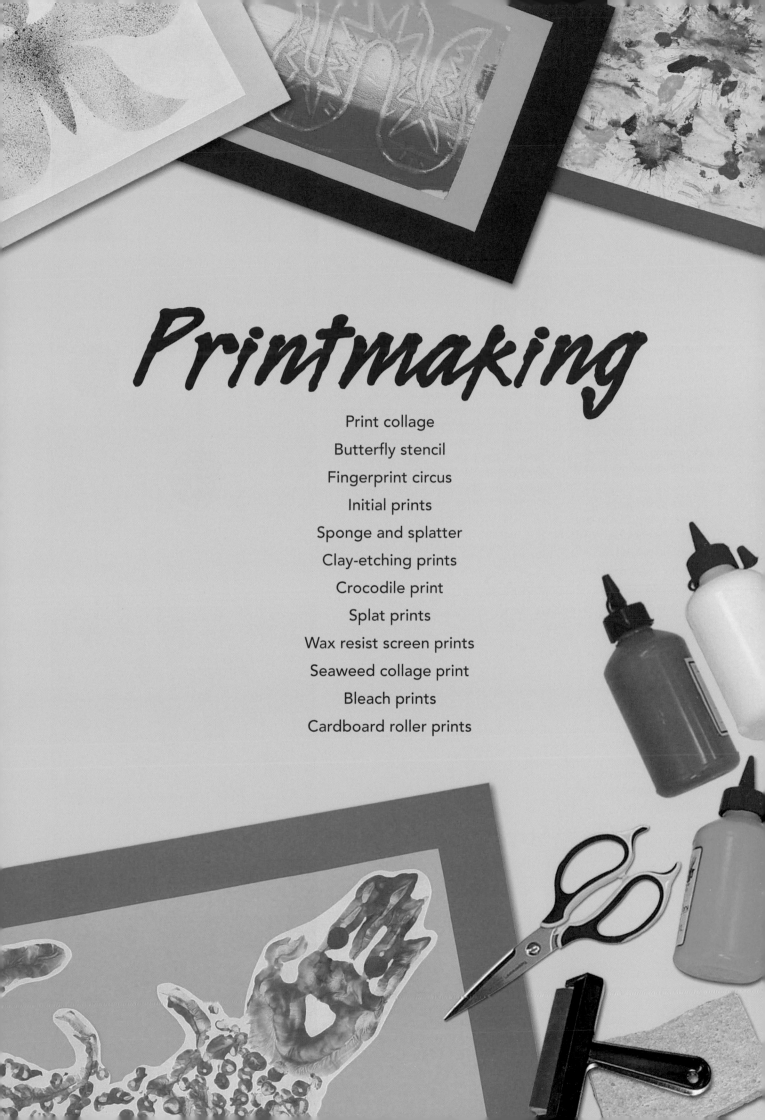

Printmaking

Print collage
Butterfly stencil
Fingerprint circus
Initial prints
Sponge and splatter
Clay-etching prints
Crocodile print
Splat prints
Wax resist screen prints
Seaweed collage print
Bleach prints
Cardboard roller prints

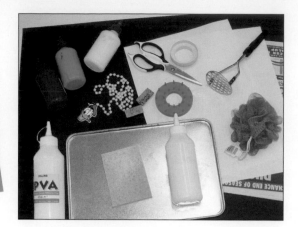

Resources
- household items
- newspaper
- two sheets of white paper
- paint in primary colours
- white paint
- black card for mounting
- scissors and glue
- black felt-tipped pen
- tray
- sponge

Indications:

Skills, techniques, technologies and processes

- Combines different kinds of prints to create a print collage.
- Creates artwork using the prints of household objects.

Responding, reflecting on and evaluating visual arts

- Looks at household objects and discusses their potential as tools for creating art.
- Selects everyday items that make interesting prints.

Inspiration

- Make a collection of household objects. Discuss the kinds of prints the objects would make.
- Select students to demonstrate how each of the objects could be used to make a print.
- Invite the students to bring interesting household objects suitable for printing to share.

Instructions

Step 1

Collect a number of household items you think will make interesting prints. Prepare a work area with newspaper or plastic sheeting. Ensure the students are wearing protecting clothing. Pour yellow, red and blue paint onto a tray and dip one of the household items selected into one of the paint colours. Make a print of the household item several times on a sheet of white paper. Repeat this process using the other household items, alternating between the three paint colours.

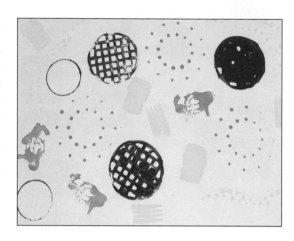

Step 2

Using the same three colours in the tray, print onto a second piece of white paper using a shower or sea sponge. Cover the page and allow the prints to overlap and mix to create secondary colours in places. Allow the sponge prints to dry.

Step 3

When the household prints are dry, carefully cut around each one leaving a very narrow margin of white paper. Take the time to cut out intricate areas, as this will enhance the final collage.

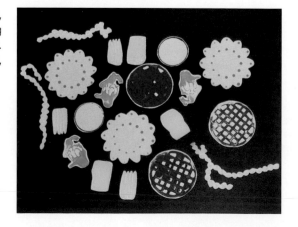

Print collage

Step 4 Arrange the cut-out household prints on the sponge print background, randomly, or in a pattern. Use strong glue to fasten the cut-outs to their designated places. Mount against a black background.

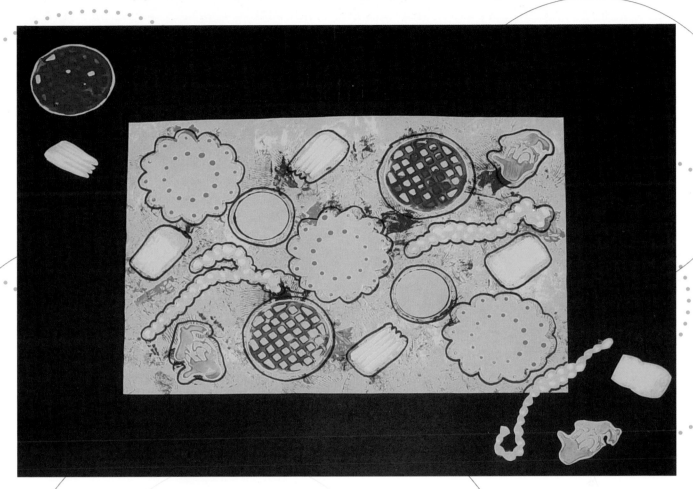

Variations

- Give three or four students a different household item to print. Students print their item in sequence in a spiral pattern on a large sheet of paper.
- Make collages using the prints of items found in the garden or school.
- Make print patterns and collages using different types of food.

Reflections

- Name the household items you used to make prints with. Why did you choose these objects?
- Can you tell what each of the prints was made by?
- How did you arrange the cut-out prints on the sponge printed background? Did you follow a pattern?
- Do you think your prints make an interesting piece of artwork?

Cross-curricular activities

- Students take turns to select criteria to sort household objects.
- Investigate kitchen utensils and how they are used. Provide utensils for the students to use during role-play activities.
- Follow instructions to cook something simple. Use a variety of cooking utensils in the process.
- Invent a household item which makes a chore easier. For example, an easy way to wash a dog.

Resources

- red, yellow, blue, green, purple and orange paint
- paint palette
- toothbrush
- newspaper
- white paper
- lead pencil
- blue card for mounting
- scissors and glue

Indications:

Skills, techniques, technologies and processes

- Designs and draws half of a butterfly with a view to creating a whole symmetrical butterfly.
- Uses a toothbrush to create a uniform spray-paint pattern.

Responding, reflecting on and evaluating visual arts

- Enjoys creating a unique symmetrical butterfly stencil through folding and cutting.

Inspiration

- Give the students objects to cut from folded paper. The whole object should be revealed when opened out. Examples may include trees, people, buildings and insects.
- Look at pictures of butterflies. Note the symmetrical colour distribution and patterning.
- Allow the students to experiment with spray painting using a toothbrush.

Instructions

Step 1

Fold a sheet of white paper in half. Imagine a complete butterfly shape. Consider the style of lines used to create the butterfly. Will they be flowing or angular? Students picture the butterfly in their mind and draw half of the design outline so the centre of the butterfly's body sits flush against the fold line.

Step 2

While the paper is still folded, carefully cut along the drawn line, being sure not to cut into or damage the outside section of paper. When finished cutting, open out the butterfly and the 'cut away' section of the paper. Discard the butterfly shape and keep the cut away or outside section of paper. This will become the stencil.

Step 3

Prepare a work area with newspaper or plastic sheeting. Ensure the students are wearing protective clothing. Lay the butterfly stencil directly on top of another sheet of white paper. It is helpful to use a sheet the same size as the stencil as this will help to keep the stencil aligned for printing. Pour small amounts of each of the paints onto a palette. Dip the bristles of a toothbrush into one of the colours and choose a part of the butterfly to apply the colour to. To ensure the butterfly remains symmetrical, spray the colour in the same place on both halves of the print. Repeat this process for each of the colours. Remove the stencil while the paint is still wet, being careful not to smudge the spray print.

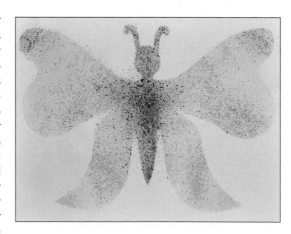

Butterfly stencil

Step 4   Allow the butterfly print to dry. Mount the print against a pastel 'blue sky' background. The stencil itself can also be quite beautiful and can also be mounted to illustrate a negative/positive image and to demonstrate the process used to create the butterfly.

Reflections

- How would you describe the shape of your butterfly? Did it unfold to reveal the butterfly shape you had intended?
- Did you spray paint your butterfly symmetrically?
- Is your butterfly print dominated by any colour(s) in particular?
- Did you achieve a clean edge for your shape using the stencil? How could you overcome any difficulties encountered in this regard?

Variations

- Make stencils of other non-symmetrical objects using litho paper and a cutting knife. (This needs to be closely supervised and assisted by adults.)
- Use a sponge to print small shapes. Repeat the stencil prints to create patterns.
- Use pre-made stencils such as lettering stencils and felt-tipped pens, to write titles or names.

Cross-curricular activities

- Identify two-dimensional and three-dimensional objects which are symmetrical.
- Draw lines of symmetry on two-dimensional shapes. Note shapes with two or more lines of symmetry.
- Make shapes which are symmetrical by folding and cutting.
- Add split pins to 2-D shapes with rotational symmetry. Demonstrate rotational symmetry by tracing and turning the shape.
- Investigate the life span and cycle of a butterfly.

Resources

- tray
- newspaper
- black card for mounting
- red, yellow, orange paint
- red and yellow paper squares
- red, brown, orange and black felt-tipped pens
- scissors and glue
- white paper
- aluminium foil

Indications:

Skills, techniques, technologies and processes

- Makes fingerprints and uses them to create imaginary acrobats.
- Combines printmaking, drawing and collage to create a multi-media artwork.

Responding, reflecting on and evaluating visual arts

- Uses imagination to transform simple fingerprints into cartoon-style figures.
- Uses collage to create a vibrant festive image.

Inspiration

- Brainstorm to list the types of people and acts that can be seen at circuses. Discuss acrobatic and gymnastic acts in particular.
- Give the students large sheets of butcher's paper. Allow them to make colourful fingerprints and thumb prints all over the page, and, when dry, create little characters by adding detail with felt-tipped pens.

Instructions

Step 1

Prepare a work area with newspaper or plastic sheeting. Ensure the students are wearing protective clothing. Pour red, orange and yellow paint onto a tray or palette. Prepare sheets of white, red and yellow paper onto which to print. Dip a finger into one of the paint colours and make several prints with a single paint application onto one of the sheets of paper. Clean that finger or use another to make prints on the paper in the other two colours. Note that red should not be printed onto red paper or yellow on yellow paper as they will not be seen clearly. Allow the fingerprints to dry.

Step 2

Visualise characters found at a circus and the activities they might perform. Use coloured felt-tipped pens to add details to the fingerprints and transform them into little circus characters. Some of the fingerprints should also take on the role of audience members. Cut around each of the figures drawn.

Step 3

Cut out sections of yellow and red paper to create a 'big top'. Lay the pieces on black mounting card along with the circus figures arranged in suitable positions. Other accessories can be drawn, cut out and added to complete the scene.

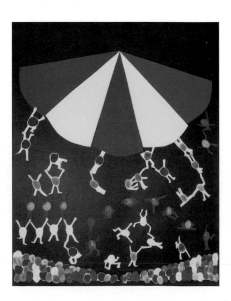

Fingerprint circus

Step 4

When satisfied with the layout of the circus, glue each piece into position. Add pieces of aluminium foil to represent bright light to complete the scene. Lighting can be further enhanced by covering the aluminium foil in red or yellow cellophane.

Reflections

- What characters did you include in your circus picture? Which of the characters are your favourites?

- Were your prints clear? What made your prints unique?

- What other pictures could be created using fingerprints or other body prints?

- What else did you add or could you add to enhance the circus atmosphere of your picture?

Variations

- Use fingerprints to create a 'stone wall' or similar textures to form pictures such as buildings or bridges.

- Use fingerprint characters to decorate gift tags for Christmas presents.

- Use either body parts such as feet, toes and hands to create prints of native animals or birds. Enhance with felt-tipped pens or a fine paintbrush.

Cross-curricular activities

- Investigate and discuss how circuses have changed overtime; e.g. the treatment of animals.

- Hold gymnastics classes where the students can learn and practise simple circus-style activities.

- Ask the students to work in small groups or pairs to invent the 'Greatest circus on earth'. Describe the setting and write an order of performance.

- Students illustrate an advertisement for their imaginary circus.

Resources
- fluorescent paints
- white paper
- hard roller
- thick cardboard squares
- thin soft rope or thick string
- navy card for mounting
- scissors and strong glue
- tray
- newspaper
- lead pencil

Indications:

Skills, techniques, technologies and processes

- Cuts, shapes and glues sections of string into a stylised shape of a letter.

- Uses a string collage as a print block.

Responding, reflecting on and evaluating visual arts

- Understands the reversal that occurs when an object is printed and takes this into consideration when creating a print block.

- Appreciates their own letter design as unique and representative of something about themselves.

Inspiration

- Encourage the students to write their initials in a variety of different ways and choose the one they find most interesting or appealing. Experiment with both straight and curved line fonts.

- Brainstorm a list of places an initial print could be used.

- Look at stamps made with a particular message such as those used by businesses.

Instructions

Step 1

Students draw a stylised version of the initial of their first name. Think about the types of lines they could use. What image do they want to portray about themselves through their art? Consider the mirror effect that occurs when printing takes place. Think about what will happen when some letters are reversed. Determine whether their initial will need to be drawn in reverse in order to print correctly. Then draw their letter onto a piece of heavy card using lead pencil.

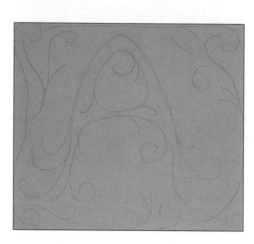

Step 2

Prepare a work area with newspaper or plastic sheeting. Ensure the students are wearing protective clothing. Cut a variety of lengths of thick string. Apply strong glue onto the lines of the drawing and add the string. (Many lengths of string can be combined to create some thicker lines). When all lines have been covered with string, allow the glue to dry. This may take some time.

Step 3

Pour three colours of paint side by side onto a tray. Use a hard roller to mix the bands together slightly and create a smooth surface. Press the string side of the printing card into the paint on the tray and roll the back of the card with a hard roller to ensure all parts of the string have picked up the paint evenly. Carefully pick up the printing card and place it face down onto a sheet of white paper. Alternatively, use a paintbrush to apply coloured paints to the string on the print block. Use a hard roller to roll across the back of the printing card, ensuring all sections of the string have been printed evenly. Carefully remove the printing card to reveal the print.

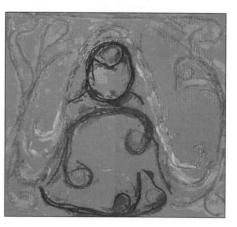

Initial prints

Step 4 Allow the print to dry. Display against a navy background or make several prints and mount them onto the front covers of school books.

Reflections

- How did you get the string in place? Did the final initials hold the shape you intended?
- What colour (or colours) did you choose to make your print? Did you use special paper or borders to enhance your print?
- Where did you use your initial prints?
- How would you describe the style of your lettering?

Variations

- Experiment with special decorative writing to write initials. These could be invented or copied from calligraphy books. Give the students a variety of writing implements to use.
- Use string to create patterns suitable for continuous borders when printed end to end.
- Glue other materials suitable for collages to a wood block to create a variety of textures for printing.

Cross-curricular activities

- Brainstorm to list words or company names that are commonly reduced to initials.
- Introduce acronyms to the students. Students invent acronyms for sayings that are familiar to them.
- Students write acrostic poems for their own names or for the name of something recently studied.
- Give the students opportunities to look at and attempt to complete forms such as bank slips where a signature is required.

Resources
- toothbrush
- sponges
- tray
- red, blue, purple and white paint
- large sheets of white paper
- paper for square templates
- newspaper
- scissors

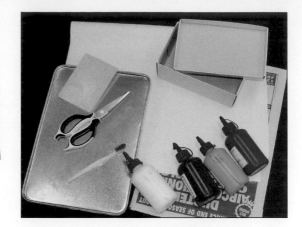

Indications:

Skills, techniques, technologies and processes

- Creates simple templates.
- Sponges and splatters paint around a template to reveal a shape's boundaries.

Responding, reflecting on and evaluating visual arts

- Recognises that a template can be used in a number of ways to create a print.
- Varies the number and arrangement of templates depending on the technique used for printing.

Inspiration

- Brainstorm to find ways for creating squares on a page. Suggest drawing, printing, stencilling and so on.
- Students experiment with different techniques for creating perfect squares on a large sheet of butcher's paper.
- Look at the colour wheel and identify analogous colours (two or three colours side by side on the colour wheel). Encourage the students to describe these colour groups in terms of warmth.

Instructions

Step 1

Cut several squares from a sheet of paper to create different-sized square templates. Place the square templates across the sheet of paper to be printed in a balanced manner. Balance can be achieved by spreading the squares evenly across the page rather than grouping them all in one area. Prepare a work area with newspaper or plastic sheeting. Ensure the students are wearing protecting clothing. Pour a small amount of red paint onto a palette or tray and dip the bristles of a toothbrush into it. Carefully flick the paint off the toothbrush onto the page with the square templates. Flick paint onto all parts of the page, so each square is surrounded by the splattered paint. While the paint is still wet, carefully remove each of the squares and allow the squares and the printed page to dry.

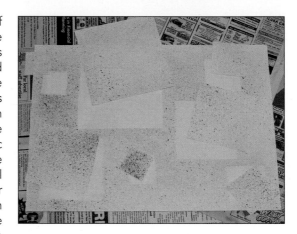

Step 2

Arrange the squares on the page again in different positions. Again, position the squares so they are balanced across the page. Pour a small amount of purple paint onto a palette or tray and dab a sponge into the paint. Holding down a square, carefully dab the sponge around the boundary of the square and then remove the templates. Allow the squares and the printed page to dry.

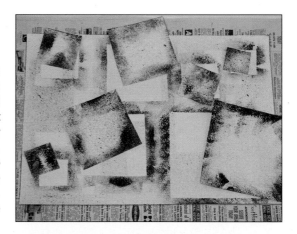

Step 3

Pour a small amount of blue paint onto a tray and use a sponge to apply paint to one of the squares. Press the square evenly onto the printed page in a selected position and repeat with other squares to create a balanced image. Remove the squares while the paint is still wet.

Sponge and splatter

Step 4 When the paper has dried, use it as a wrapping paper to cover a present. Add curling ribbon to complete the wrapping. Alternatively, mount the print against a bright colour and display.

Reflections

- What types of stencilling and printing did you incorporate into your wrapping paper?
- Which techniques stand out? Which look most effective?
- What colours did you choose? Are they analogous colours?
- How would you describe the colours you chose in terms of warmth?
- What occasion do you think your wrapping paper would best be suited for?

Variations

- Glue layers of tissue paper and cellophane squares over a three-dimensional surface such as a box and transform it into a colourful storage unit.
- Use stencil-printed wrapping paper to cover books.
- Trace around printed squares using gold and silver crayon or pens to enhance the design.
- Add seasonal words to stencil-printed wrapping paper in decorative writing using gold and silver pens.
- Repeat the process using other shapes.

Cross-curricular activities

- Find the perimeters and areas of squares and rectangles.
- Look at how squares are combined to make nets of cubes.
- Use dot paper to construct squares of different sizes and develop an understanding of square numbers.
- Use grid paper to create graphs where each square represents a given unit.

Resources

- paintbrush
- newspaper
- white paper
- green card for mounting
- scissors and glue
- green and brown paper squares
- green, blue and brown paint
- etching tools
- clay
- tray

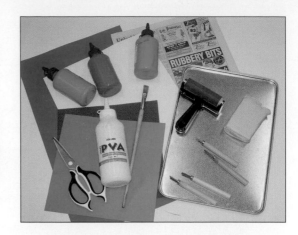

Indications:

Skills, techniques, technologies and processes

- Etches a simple design into clay to create a print block.
- Paints a number of colours on a print block to create a single print.

Responding, reflecting on and evaluating visual arts

- Develops a personal criteria for what makes a good print.
- Makes several prints from one paint application and selects the best print based on personal criteria.

Inspiration

- Encourage the students to choose a subject to draw and develop it through a series of drawings into something simplified and suitable for printing.
- Allow the students to handle clay and practise etching using carving tools or from objects such as toothpicks, plastic cutlery or plastic straws. Encourage the students to develop techniques that will give them a clean and precise finish in the clay.

Instructions

Step 1

Prepare a work area with newspaper or plastic sheeting. Ensure the students are wearing protective clothing. Provide the students with clay-modelling equipment including modelling boards (heavy board covered in calico works well and will absorb excess moisture in the clay and prevent the clay sticking to the work surface) and etching tools. Form a small piece of clay into a smooth ball. Flatten the ball to create a palm-sized circle of clay. Smooth the surface and edges using fingertips. Select an etching tool and etch the design into the surface of the clay. The lines need to be deep enough to create a recess in the remaining flat clay surface. Once complete, clean away any excess clay scraps and drop the etched side of the clay onto a flat surface to remove any unwanted 'bumps'.

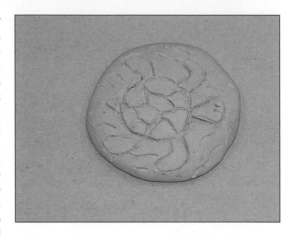

Step 2

Pour small amounts of coloured paint onto a tray. Use a paintbrush to paint each section of the etched picture on the clay.

Step 3

Print the image several times onto a sheet of white paper. Several prints can be taken from a single paint application to produce a slightly different image with each print.

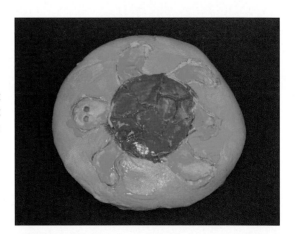

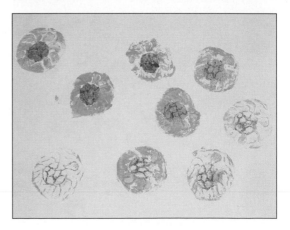

Clay-etching prints

Step 4 Select the best prints and cut them out. Glue them onto a suitable background to represent the environment in which your subject might be found. Consider using a printmaking technique to create an unusual background for your prints.

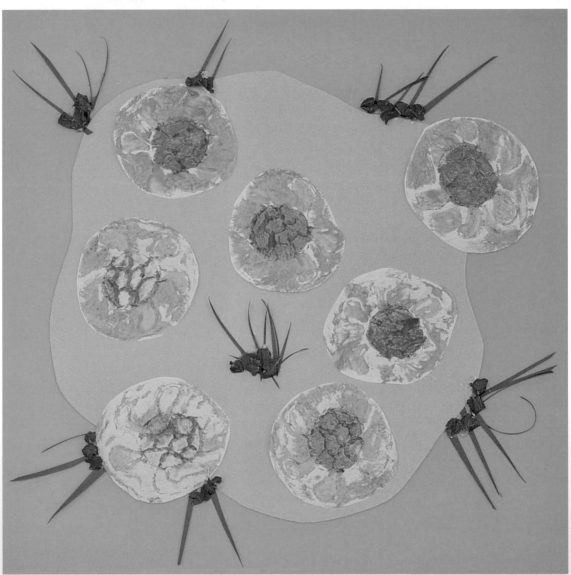

Reflections

- How did you go about achieving a clean surface for printing? What tools did you use to etch your drawing?

- Why did you choose the subject you did?

- What do you like about your design?

- Did you use more than one colour? Did this look effective?

Variations

- Etch other materials such as soft fruits or vegetables to create pictures.

- Carve pictures in soap and use as a print block.

- Make a series of clay stamps in the shapes of letters or commonly seen icons such as smiley faces.

- Build up a raised surface of clay using balls and ropes, rather than etching to create a printable surface.

Cross-curricular activities

- Find out about how newspapers are printed and the use of etched metal plates in the past.

- Write short stories about early humans and etch them into clay slabs to create 'prehistoric' writing tablets.

- Visit a printer or newspaper publishing house, or invite someone to explain to the students how printmaking happens today and the types of technology that have been developed to assist printmakers.

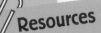

Resources

- white paper
- tray
- newspaper
- orange paper square
- dark green card for mounting
- green, orange, black and yellow paint
- scissors and glue

Indications:

Skills, techniques, technologies and processes

- Uses hands in different positions to create prints of different shapes.
- Combines different types of hand prints to create a picture of something familiar.

Responding, reflecting on and evaluating visual arts

- Thinks about where each print needs to be positioned so it fits inside the boundaries of the print surface.
- Uses imagination to see a familiar image formed from hand prints.

Inspiration

- Look at images of crocodiles. Pay special attention to the different textures on their skin and have the students suggest ways these textures could be replicated through printmaking.
- Students make an unusual print with their hand and ask others to think of what this print would depict as a whole or part of a picture.

Instructions

Step 1

Prepare a work area with newspaper or plastic sheeting. Ensure the students are wearing protective clothing. Pour green, yellow, orange and a very small amount of black paint into a swirl pattern so all colours can still be seen. Place a hand with fingers together palm down into the paint. Print the hand onto the sheet of paper. This print will represent a crocodile's broad head.

Step 2

Form a fist with the same hand and dip the knuckles into the semi-mixed paint. Use the knuckles to print the crocodile's knobbly back. These prints should extend most of the way across the page and curl downward towards the tail end. The knuckles can also be used to form a boundary on either side of the body and to create heavier ridges down the centre of the back if desired.

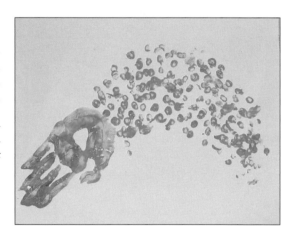

Step 3

Dip the 'pinky finger' side of the hand into the paint and curl the pinky slightly. Use the curved edge created with the edge of the hand to print a curved tail that is thicker at the palm end and narrowest at the tip of the pinky. Reapply paint to the edge of the pinky or forefinger to make short curved legs on either side of the crocodile's body. Allow to dry.

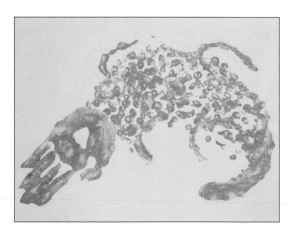

Crocodile print

Step 4   Cut shapes from orange paper to create eyes for the crocodile. Add detail to the eyes with a felt-tipped pen if desired. Mount against a dark green or brown background.

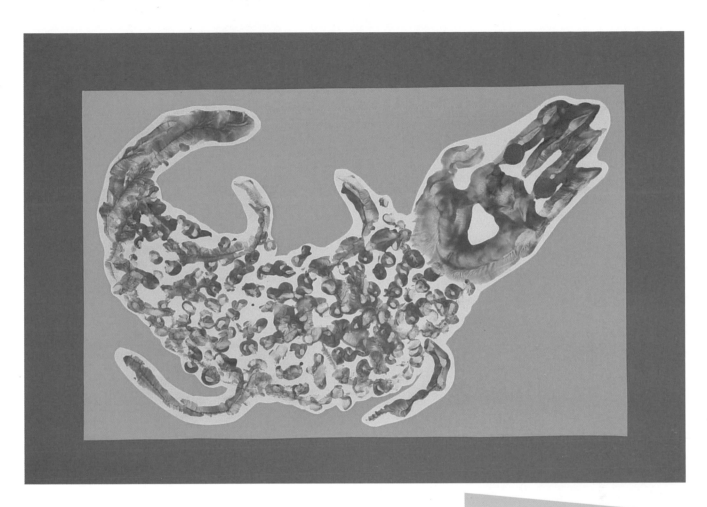

Reflections

- Does your final picture look like a crocodile? Are you pleased with the results? Did you add anything to the print to enhance the image?
- Were you able to shape your hand to create the prints you wanted? Could you create other pictures using hand prints? What would you like to attempt next?

Variations

- Use body prints to create other prehistoric creatures.
- The whole class makes multi-coloured hand prints on a large piece of material. Use the prints to represent unity, acceptance of others or multiculturalism.
- Students create tracks of an animal, using finger or partial hand prints across a page, to accompany a drawing or painting of the animal.

Cross-curricular activities

- Investigate the habitats and behaviours of crocodiles.
- Research the difference between crocodiles and alligators.
- Find out about different skin coverings and the purpose they serve.
- Brainstorm to find other creatures besides crocodiles that might live in a freshwater pond. Develop a food web using this list.

Resources

- fluorescent purple, red and green paint
- tennis ball
- white paper
- tray
- newspaper
- high-sided container e.g. ice-cream container
- red card for mounting

Indications:

Skills, techniques, technologies and processes

- Uses gravity to assist in making unusual prints.
- Uses an everyday object in an inventive way to create a print.

Responding, reflecting on and evaluating visual arts

- Looks at everyday objects as potential printmaking implements for creating art.
- Appreciates that there can be a physical aspect to some unusual artistic procedures.

Inspiration

- Look carefully at the patterns made by raindrops when they hit the ground. Use coloured water to illustrate this on scraps of butcher's paper.
- Recall situations where the students have seen a splat occur; for example, when a basketball is dropped in a puddle. Describe the types of patterns made by the water in this situation.

Instructions

Step 1

Prepare a work area with newspaper or plastic sheeting. This activity will best be performed in an outdoor area that can be easily washed or hosed down afterwards. Ensure the students are wearing protective clothing. Pour fluorescent paints onto a tray and roll a tennis ball through the paint so that the surface is covered. Roll the ball over a clean sheet of paper to create a winding linear print.

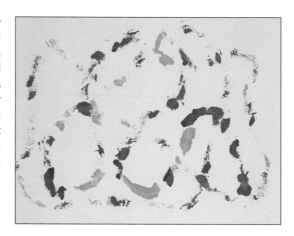

Step 2

Make a solution of two parts to one part water in a high-sided container; e.g. an ice-cream container. Prepare a large area of newspaper or plastic and place the sheet of paper previously printed with the linear design in the centre of it. Place the tennis ball in the solution so that it is completely covered and soaked with paint. Stand above the paper holding the tennis ball and attempt to 'line up' where you want the splat print to be on the page. Drop the tennis ball and then catch it after it bounces.

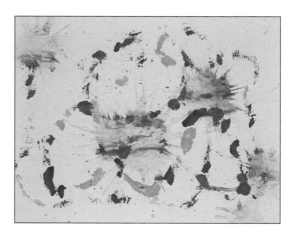

Step 3

Repeat Step 2 using other colours to create a colourful print. Lay the print on a flat surface to dry.

Splat prints

Select a colour from the print to use as a mount for your artwork. Alternatively, individual splat prints look effective when cut out carefully and used to decorate classroom displays.

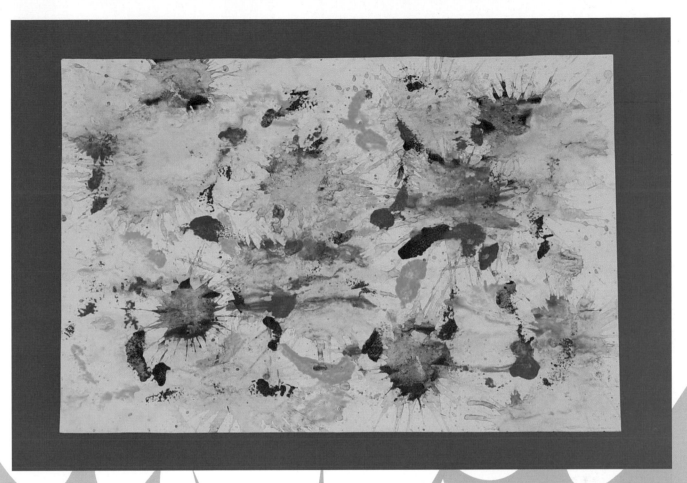

Reflections

- What kind of pattern did you make when you rolled the tennis ball across the paper?
- What kind of pattern did you make when you dropped the tennis ball on the paper? Did you catch the ball again?
- How many splat prints did you make? Was this enough to make your print look good? Were there too many?
- Did you enjoy using splat prints to make art?

Variations

- Use spray bottles to spray diluted paint at a wall of paper and create interesting prints.
- Use other types of balls, small beanbags and partially blown up balloons to create unusual splats when dropped.
- Propel the object used to make the splat print from different directions, to make elliptical splats across the page.

Cross-curricular activities

- Use tennis balls in a variety of activities to develop hand-eye coordination and improve fitness.
- Compare the properties of different balls, including weight, height of bounce and volume.
- Use a ball in a 'share circle' to determine who will share next. The students can pass or roll the ball to the next person to speak.
- Brainstorm to list team sports that use a ball. Research the origins and rules of a chosen ball game.
- Invent a new ball game including the rules and resources required.

Resources

- silk screen
- newspaper
- greasy crayon
- white paper
- squeegee
- fluorescent colour paints
- black card for mounting

Indications:

Skills, techniques, technologies and processes

- Draws an image onto a screen to create a barrier through which paint will not pass.
- Uses a squeegee to force paint through a silk screen and cover the print surface.

Responding, reflecting on and evaluating visual arts

- Identifies the best way to hold and apply paint using a squeegee.
- Suggests other ways a screen could be used to assist in printmaking.

Inspiration

- Look at prints made using a screen. Discuss how these prints are made and describe the wax resist technique the students will be using.
- Discuss the types of images that could be printed using the wax resist technique. Identify that the subject will be a line drawing with its internal areas being the same colour as its background.
- Brainstorm to list ideas for suitable subjects.

Instructions

Step 1

Place a silk screen on top of a newspaper surface. Draw a simple design lightly on a silk screen surface in pencil. Ensure that the silk screen is flat on the work surface and not suspended while drawing. When happy with the design, retrace with a greasy crayon, using several coats if necessary to create a waxy barrier through which paint will not pass.

Step 2

Prepare a work area with newspaper or plastic sheeting. Ensure the students are wearing protective clothing. Lay the silk screen carefully over a sheet of blank paper. Pour paint along the top edge of the screen. Several colours can be used if desired. Have a second person hold the screen firmly in place. Use a squeegee to drag the paint across the screen surface towards you to push the paint through to the paper. Enough pressure should be applied to the squeegee for it to flex while dragging the paint. Lift the squeegee and start again at the top. Two or three 'runs' of the squeegee may be required for the entire surface to become covered in paint.

Step 3

Carefully lift the screen to reveal the printed page. Several prints can be taken while the screen's design is intact. The screen can even be washed in between prints if a new colour scheme is required. Scrubbing the screen with detergent will remove the crayon design when complete.

Wax resist screen prints

Step 4 Allow the prints to dry. Select the best print considering both the colour scheme used and the quality and clarity of the prints. Prints will become less clear with each print 'run'. Mount on a black background for a striking display.

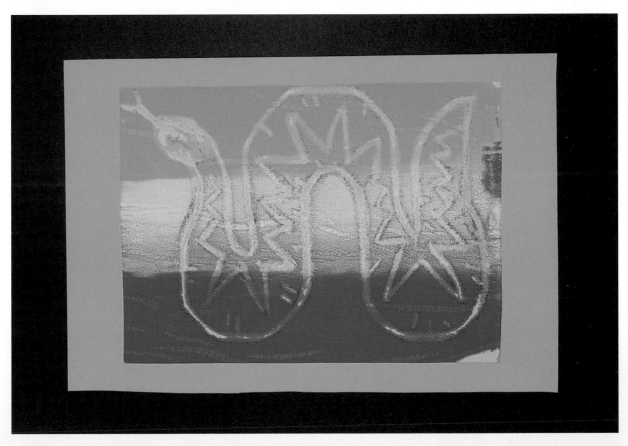

Reflections

- What did you decide to draw as your subject? Why did you think this subject would be suited to wax resist screen printing?
- What colours did you combine in your print? Where they good choices?
- Did you enjoy printing using a screen and squeegee? Did you encounter any difficulties? How did you overcome them?
- Was your print clear? How many prints did you make? Were they all successful? What made one better than another?

Variations

- Use a stencil to print through a silk screen. Simple stencils can be made by folding a sheet of lithograph paper in half and cutting away an internal design.
- Drip melted wax onto the screen in an interesting pattern or follow a shape drawn onto paper and placed underneath the screen as a guide.
- Use wax resist designs to print T-shirts and library bags.

Cross-curricular activities

- Investigate uses for screens other than printmaking.
- Identify other forms of screens and their uses. For example, netting for catching fish or sifters used to separate flour from husks.
- Imagine one of the prints you made is the cover of a CD. What would be on the CD? Add text and other detail to create a complete cover design.

Resources
- seaside collage materials
- heavy cardboard
- paintbrush
- strong glue
- soft roller
- green, brown, and yellow paint
- dark blue card for mounting
- tray
- newspaper

Indications:

Skills, techniques, technologies and processes

- Selects and creates a collage of seaside materials with interesting textures suitable for print making.
- Makes a print from a relief collage.

Responding, reflecting on and evaluating visual arts

- Anticipates what sections of a collage will require extra attention in order to print successfully.
- Uses colours that are suggestive of seaside matter.

Inspiration

- Go for an excursion to the beach and comb the beach for interesting 'bits and pieces' for making a collage.
- Identify living and non-living elements on the shoreline. Use this as part of the criteria to decide what to take home for their collage.
- Look at interesting formations created by interactions between water, sand and seaweed along the shoreline.

Instructions

Step 1

Collect a variety of seaside materials including seaweed, sea sponges, dune vegetation, driftwood, small shells, cuttlefish shells and fishing line. *Ensure that all items collected are not living.* Prepare a work area with newspaper or plastic sheeting. Ensure the students are wearing protective clothing. Glue the seaside materials onto a piece of thick card. Allow time for the collage to dry. This may take some time.

Step 2

Pour 'seaweed' coloured paints (brown, green, yellow) onto a tray and use a soft roller to combine the paints. Use the roller to pick up the paint and roll it onto the surface of the collage. If some sections of the collage are difficult to sponge paint, use a paintbrush to assist in covering all of the materials. Turn the collage over and carefully place on top of a second sheet of paper. Press heavily over all parts of the card to ensure each item in the collage prints clearly.

Step 3

Carefully lift off the collage to reveal the print. Allow the print to dry. Add extra materials such as small shells or strands of seaweed to the print to enhance the seaside effect.

Seaweed collage print

Step 4   Allow the materials to dry. If desired, paint sections of the print with liquid starch and sprinkle with sand. Mount against a dark blue sea background.

Reflections

- Were you able to find some interesting seaside 'bits and pieces' for your collage? What criteria did you use to decide what things to include in your collage?
- What things did you think would make the most interesting print? Were your predictions correct?
- How did you use the collage materials and sand to complement your final print? Do you think these were good additions or did they dominate your artwork and detract from the print you made?

Variations

- Choose one seaside element to make a repeat print pattern.
- Make a single print of a seaside element and transform it into something from another environment by drawing details in felt-tipped pen. For example, print a piece of flat coral and transform it into a tree.
- Use vibrant colours to print your collage and create a coral reef.

Cross-curricular activities

- Conduct a seaside investigation, including an analysis of beach debris and case studies of environmental issues such as dune erosion.
- Brainstorm to list the habitats that exist within a marine environment. List the living and non-living elements in each of these habitats.
- Write a story about a worm on a fishhook and its death-defying escape.
- Compare uses for salt water and fresh water.

Resources

- red edicol dye
- paper towel
- white paper
- wide paintbrush
- white and red card for mounting
- plant leaves with intricate foliage
- protective disposable gloves
- newspaper
- bleach
- tray

Indications:

Skills, techniques, technologies and processes

- Applies bleach to a print surface in place of paint to remove colour and create a printed image.
- Employs safety measures when using chemicals.

Responding, reflecting on and evaluating visual arts

- Recognises that bleach can be used to remove colour.
- Suggests other applications for using bleach in artworks.

Inspiration

- Provide the students with a number of two-toned images to view; e.g. those using two colours of blue or silhouettes.
- Illustrate the effect of bleach upon everyday objects; e.g. a fabric scrap or tissue paper. Discuss how bleach could be used to create a two-toned image.
- Brainstorm to list materials that could be used to make a print using bleach. Note that they will need to be disposable as the bleach will damage the materials used.

Instructions

Step 1

Prepare a work area with newspaper or plastic sheeting. Ensure the students are wearing protective clothing. Prepare a solution of red edicol dye. Use a wide paintbrush to paint a sheet of white paper with the dye. Allow the dye to dry.

Step 2

Select leaves with intricate foliage to print (conifers and ferns will create the most interesting prints). Put on protective disposable gloves and pour a small amount of bleach into a high-sided tray. Note that bleach will strip colour out of fabrics, paper and hair. Avoid contact with the skin. You will need enough bleach to cover the foliage of the leaves. Break the foliage apart to create several single-layered sections to print. Dip a frond into the bleach. Remove the frond and hold it over paper towels for a short time to remove excess bleach.

Step 3

Lay the frond on the dyed paper and leave it there. Repeat the process for each of the fronds until the dyed paper is covered in an arrangement of fronds. Gently press down on each of the fronds to ensure all parts of the foliage have made contact with the paper. Carefully remove the foliage to reveal the bleach print. Allow the surface to dry. Take care when cleaning the tray that the bleach does not come into contact with anything that could become bleached and damaged. Carefully remove the gloves and dispose of them.

Bleach prints

Step 4 Mount the print against a bright red background to display. Alternatively, cut the prints into small sections and glue onto folded pieces of card to make striking red greeting cards for Christmas.

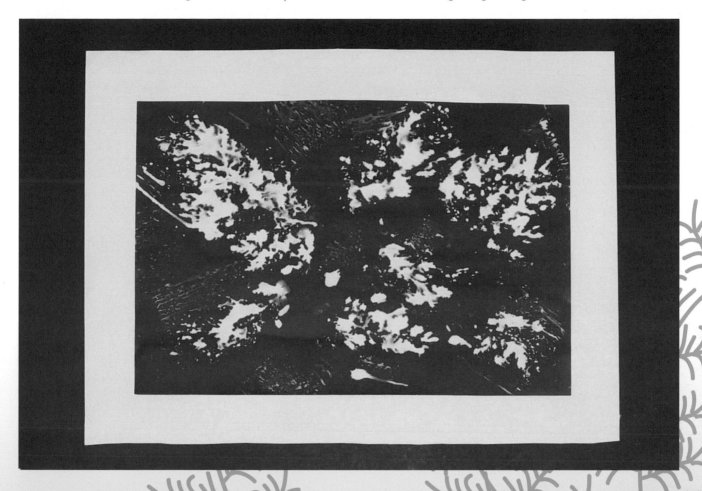

Variations

- Bleach prints onto tissue paper or brightly coloured fabric.
- Use bleach to draw pictures onto coloured paper using cotton tips.
- Use bleach in place of paint when printing on the surface of a collage.

Reflections

- What plant leaves did you choose to print? Why did you choose this plant?
- Did the bleach make the print you anticipated? How is it different?
- Do you like the print your plant made? Does it still resemble a plant? How would you describe its form?
- Do you think bleach is an effective medium to use in printmaking? How does it differ from paint?

Cross-curricular activities

- Investigate the way the sun bleaches things left outdoors. Make a display of items that have become bleached by the sun.
- Define what is meant by 'hazardous' and 'poisonous.' Identify things around the house that are hazardous or poisonous.
- Discuss the impact using harmful chemicals might have on the environment.

Resources

- cardboard tube
- white paper
- black card for mounting
- fabric and textured scraps
- hard roller/straight-edged tool
- fluorescent purple paint, black paint and white paint
- scissors and strong glue
- newspaper
- sponges
- tray

Indications:

Skills, techniques, technologies and processes

- Glues materials onto a cardboard cylinder to create a print roller.
- Creates continuous prints using a print roller.

Responding, reflecting on and evaluating visual arts

- Thinks about what kind of continuous pattern they could create using a roller.
- Identifies places in real life where rollers are an efficient means of printing.

Inspiration

- Provide continuous patterns for the students to view e.g. wallpaper and curtain fabric.
- Demonstrate the continuous nature of a roller by making lines of two different colours on either side of a sponge roller and rolling it across a sheet of scrap paper.
- Discuss the types of continuous patterns that could be created using a roller.
- Provide a wide variety of materials for the student to handle and brainstorm continuous texture ideas.

Instructions

Step 1

Collect a variety of fabric and other textured scraps suitable for printing. Prepare a work area with the newspaper or plastic sheeting. Ensure the students are wearing protective clothing. Cut out sections of the scraps as desired and use strong glue to adhere the scraps in a pattern around the cardboard. Consider what the roller print will look like as each piece is glued onto the roller. Allow time to dry.

Step 2

Pour purple, black and white paint onto a tray in lines side by side. Use a hard roller or a straight-edged tool to join the colours together and blend them at the edges. Carefully place the tube at one end of the paint tray and roll it across the paint, picking up as much paint on the roller as possible.

Step 3

Place the paint-covered tube at one end of a sheet of white paper and slowly roll it from end of the paper to the other. Be careful not to slide the roller so smudging does not occur. Repeat the rolling on any part of the page that has been missed by rolling parallel to the original print.

Cardboard roller prints

Step 4 While the paint is still wet, glitter or other types of 'sparkle' can be added. Allow the print to dry and mount against a black background. If all students in the class are using the same size roller, the patterns can be combined to make a large class roller print on a length of butcher's paper. Each student can place his/her roller print directly below the previous student's to create a pattern wall.

Reflections

- What materials did you decide to glue onto your roller? Why did you choose these materials?
- What texture effects did you aim to achieve?
- How did you go about making the roller prints? Did you encounter any difficulties?
- Was your print a success? What made it successful or unsuccessful?

Variations

- Paint a sponge roller with several colours in a continuous design using a paintbrush. Roll onto paper strips to create a fancy border for displays.
- Form rollers out of clay and etch a design into the clay to print.
- Make a block print with a design that can 'join up' at the same point on either edge. Join several block prints together to make a continuous print.

Cross-curricular activities

- Use the senses to explore different textures including natural and human-made objects.
- Explore patterns in numbers. Find missing numbers and extend number patterns.
- Students create their own number pattern for their peers to decode and extend.
- Identify animals with distinctive patterning on their body and discover why the patterning is important.

Glossary – Printmaking

analogous colours	two or more colours occurring side by side on the colour wheel
calligraphy	beautiful handwriting
collage	a picture made from paper, cloth and other materials glued onto card or board
developmental drawings	a series of drawings using a variety of different techniques which explore a single subject
fonts	different styles of lettering
lithograph paper	paper produced for the purpose of printmaking with one smooth ink-repellent surface and one absorbent surface
personal criteria	a set of personally developed guidelines by which to assess
relief collage	collage where a surface is built with varying heights and textures suitable for printmaking
rotational symmetry	a pattern formed by replicating objects in a circular rotation
rubbing	reproduced patterns or designs created by rubbing paper layed over a surface with a soft medium such as chalk
silk screen	silk stretched across a wooden frame to form a fine gauze through which to print
squeegee	flexible flat-edged tool used for spreading paint at an even consistency
stencil	thin sheet of paper or other material in which lettering or other designs are cut out of it
stylised	artistic representation conformed to the rules of a conventional style
subject	something chosen by an artist for painting
template	a pre-cut cardboard design used as a guide for drawing or cutting out a closed shape
two-tone	having two colours
wax resist	the process of creating an image in wax and painting over it
wood block or lino cut	using a smooth level of block wood or linoleum, unwanted parts are cut away, and the parts left are painted and used to make a print

Useful websites

Artists and art movements

Andy Warhol and Van Gogh	www.ezmuseum.com
The Museum of Modern Art	www.moma.org
The worldwide art gallery	www.theartgallery.com.au
Textiles	www.museumfortextiles.on.ca/

Tools and techniques

Dictionary of printmaking	www.philaprintshop.com/diction.html
Colour museum	www.colour-experience.org
ArtLex on collage	www.artlex.com/
The art of marbling	members.aol.com/marbling/marbling/

Art Education

The incredible art department	www.princetonol.com/groups/iad/